5/72 II   8 25

Bruce K. Crockett
$55.00

A New Learning Environment

A Case for Learning

Harold L. Cohen
James Filipczak

Forewords by R. Buckminster Fuller
B. F. Skinner

A New Learning Environment

Jossey-Bass Inc., Publishers
San Francisco · Washington · London · 1971

A NEW LEARNING ENVIRONMENT
A Case for Learning
        by Harold L. Cohen and James Filipczak

Copyright © 1971 by Jossey-Bass, Inc., Publishers

Published in Great Britain by
Jossey-Bass, Inc., Publishers
St. George's House
44 Hatton Garden, London E.C.1

Library of Congress Catalogue Card Number LC 70-151108

International Standard Book Number ISBN 0-87589-101-2

Manufactured in the United States of America

JACKET DESIGN BY HELEN WEBBER, BERKELEY

FIRST EDITION

Code 7127

The Jossey-Bass
Behavioral Science Series

General Editors

WILLIAM E. HENRY
University of Chicago

NEVITT SANFORD
Wright Institute, Berkeley

To the present generation
of American youth

R. Buckminster Fuller

Foreword

*H*arold Cohen and James Filipczak have written about designing and managing an educational-social system. The text is full of methodology and creative science. Since I share the foreword with B. F. Skinner, I would like to use my half to describe Harold Cohen, a man I have known and worked with for over twenty years. Harold Cohen is a very sensitive man. He is also a very intuitive man. He writes a great deal about methodology; and there is a great deal about that methodology in this book. But what is most important about Cohen is, I am sure, his intuition. This does not make what he has to say about methodology unimportant, but it is important in reading *A New Learning Environment* to realize how intuitively Cohen operates.

A half a century, even a quarter of a century ago, intuition was almost a naughty word in the world of academic science, in fact in the whole world of philosophers. Pragmatism of the highest kind came in with the great Depression. Some of the validity of the out-and-out Marxian pragmatism was very convincing to many thinkers in the depths of the Depression. Many of these thinkers thought of intuition as pure romanticism and as the antithesis of pragmatism. Therefore the idea that one could get any value out of intuitions was considered as nonsensical as the idea of getting anything of value out of superstitions.

Foreword

A little over a decade ago, John Howard Northrop at Yale made a contribution of high order when he studied carefully the writings of a half dozen great scientists. He picked scientists who have made magnificent contributions, and he studied their writings, diaries, personal accounts, and personal letters. He read letters and diaries of families, all the records produced at the time the scientists were about to make their great discoveries but before they made those discoveries or knew they were going to make them. He followed the personal literature which documents the thinkings and feelings and sensations of each individual scientist about to make a great discovery, and he followed the literature through the moment of the discovery and into the months immediately following.

Northrop was interested in finding in that literature some commonality about what brought about the great discoveries of those individuals. And he found just such a commonality. Every one of those scientists made it clear in their diaries, letters, and family conversations that the number one item leading to their success was their intuition. They also then made it very clear that this intuition—this extraordinary realization of a relationship operating in the universe—suddenly, lucidly revealed to them the existence of very extraordinary generalized principles which would hold true in every special case.

It also was documented as common to all of these great scientists that the second most important item in relation to their discovery and its conversion to the advantage of humanity was their second intuition. The second intuition—what they ought to do about the discovery—came within seconds after the first. Time and time again scientists find retrospectively that they had the very same vision and awareness as another scientist who was accredited with the discovery, but they did not do anything about it. They thought they were going to do something about it sometime, but instead they just lit their pipes or went off and forgot about it.

So we have then these two important points in the life of the individuals who made the greatest scientific contributions to society—the first intuition, which was the discovery, and the second intuition, which was what to do about the discovery. Every one of these scientists said also that it does not make much difference what method you use after you have this intuition. Any method will do just so long as you are methodical—methodology is not success. We find then that what is taught at school academically in the way of method is secondary and has nothing to do with original discoveries, original contributions, or anything we call creativity.

I simply say then that Harold Cohen is—because of his very high degree of sensitivity—a most extraordinary demonstration of intuition about his fellow men. The sensitivity he was born with was never hurt. He is able to say today spontaneously the kinds of things that little children say in looking at what they see. He does not tend to deceive himself, to see through the eyes of others, or to see things conventionally.

Harold Cohen has done a great deal of experimental work. He did not know certainly that he was going to be engaged in behavioral science research. When he was first my student in Chicago at the Institute of Design in 1949, he hoped to become some kind of industrial designer. While going to school he had taught night school to children; he was always interested in teaching. He graduated from the Institute and started teaching there. A number of years later Harold was asked to go to Southern Illinois University to inaugurate a design school, and he asked me to come there and lecture. I watched Harold dealing not only with the students but with the faculty, the officers, and the president of the university. Every one of them became interested in Harold as a personality, in his extraordinary intuitive flashes. I watched him with his students in school and in his organization of the school. His organization was nowhere as interesting as the fact that Harold was always an extraordinary leader of the students. They realized that he understood their personal problems. He gave them a chance to develop themselves.

Harold became convinced of the consequences of environmental control. I think I may have had a little to do with this. Many years earlier I had committed myself to always undertaking to solve problems by changing the environment to make it more favorable to life and to the realization of the life drives, instead of by trying to reform the individual. Harold's design school was organized on the basis that he would help the individuals who came there as students to see what their problems were and to see how those problems could be solved by environmental reform instead of individual reform.

Harold Cohen began to discover in this behavioral science work that punishments break up communication and rewards bring about improved communication. He began to utilize this principle in an experiment that was made a school task, and other scientists have employed it in important ways. The intuitions that I spoke about began to play a very important part. Harold's sensitivity to other human beings enables him to perceive whether they have been punished or rewarded and to discern how to help an individual—without his knowing it—to get what he wants in the way of education.

Harold designed an experimental school as an experimental freshman year at Southern Illinois University. He had sixty-six special students who were picked out of what is called the "lower one-third." In Illinois, as in many other states, any student who graduates from high school is entitled to go to a state university. Unfortunately the capacity of state universities in Illinois is not adequate for the number of graduates. Therefore, some have to be turned down. About a third of all graduates from high school cannot be accommodated. That group is called the lower one-third, and they are excluded from the state universities. Their parents represent a very powerful part of the electorate of Illinois. As such they feel they have been unjustly dealt with, particularly that their children have been unjustly dealt with. And that irritates parents much more than if they had been personally mistreated. So there is a great pushing of the legislature of Illinois to do something about it. As a consequence a number of experimental undertakings have occurred.

Harold Cohen, trying to reform environment instead of trying to reform man, saw that he might be able to develop school apparatus and procedures to help the student learn how to teach himself. So in 1961 he designed and directed the Experimental Freshman Year program. He converted an unoccupied floor in a

new reinforced concrete fireproof building. In that unfurnished, un-
paneled, and unfloored space Cohen set up a special area which
would just very temporarily suffice with temporary floorings and
so forth. He set up his own office and an office for his staff and
several other kinds of rooms.

He had a main lecture room, two kinds of lounges, and two
rather large rooms where the whole class could meet. One area
was for group work, and in the other area each student had his own
office. Each student of the sixty-six in his class had a little paper
house (an office) that had been manufactured out of corrugated
paperboard, like a very large box for a piano or a big radio. On
the walls were the periodic table of the chemical elements and maps
of the world, and there was a world globe and a very good dictionary. You found general reference works of very important kinds,
including up-to-date ones like the world almanac. There was a telephone in the room and also a very good typewriter. The room was
extremely comfortable.

The telephone was connected directly to a switchboard and
from there to the instructor's office. If a student could not find the
information he needed in his room, he could telephone the professor
for assistance. The student did not have to leave his room to get
even the most obscure information. On the walls there were all
kinds of information—not only the periodic table but charts on all
the layers of the earth and space and charts of the greatest heights
and the greatest depths to which men have gone so far. All kinds
of quick comprehensive references were provided to give the student
a very powerful sense of where he was in the universe and how to
get special information about that universe.

Each one of these little offices was absolutely independent.
The student was informed at the outset that he would not be allowed to smoke in his room. He would not be able to have music
in his room. In fact, there were only two things he was allowed
to do in his room. He was allowed to put information into his mind
—into his brain—and he was allowed to put out. He could bring
it out onto paper by drawing it or typing it, or he could put it in
by reading his books and studying his charts or his maps. If he

wanted to smoke he had to leave his room, close the door, and go out into the lounge. The lounge was right outside so it was no trouble to go out there. If he wanted music he could go out into one of the other lounges. He developed the association that the only reason he was ever in his office was to put information into his mind or to pick it out of his mind. Thus his office became an input-output facility of the very highest order. The student began to associate it with very effective use of his mind, and it began to pay off importantly.

At Southern Illinios University, Cohen met three important behavioral scientists, Israel Goldiamond, Nathan Azrin, and Teodoro Ayllon. These men opened up to Harold their field of operant psychology. He was very impressed with the work being done at Anna State Hospital, where Ayllon and Azrin were using the application of rewards and the implications of punishment. When Harold completed the Experimental Freshman Year at Southern Illinois, he left to become education director of the Institute for Behavioral Research.

Harold put this operant approach to work in Washington, D.C., at the National Training School for Boys. There he developed the CASE project with the research knowledge that he had developed at Carbondale and Chicago in combination with the work of the operant psychologists. Harold brought James Filipczak, one of his own creative graduate students, to Washington to help in designing and running the program.

This book represents the work of intuitive men. The reader of this text should go beyond the reading of the methodology with which Harold Cohen and James Filipczak are dealing and should feel for the sensitivity of their work.

B. J. Skinner ᘓᘓᘓᘓᘓᘓᘓᘓᘓᘓᘓᘓᘓᘓᘓᘓᘓ

Foreword

ᘓᘓᘓᘓᘓᘓᘓᘓᘓᘓᘓᘓᘓᘓᘓᘓᘓᘓᘓᘓ

*W*hat does a nation do with its teen-age armed robbers, rapists, and murderers? It locks them up to punish them and to keep them from robbing, raping, or killing again. But for how long and under what conditions? And what happens afterward? It is generally agreed that incarceration is not only to protect society and punish wrongdoing but to change the offender. It is to "rehabilitate" him. For the young offender the place of incarceration is called a training school. But what is learned in it, and how is it taught?

In all schools students learn a great deal from each other. In the training school the young offender will learn that there are many others like him in the world, and with some of them he will make friends. It is not unlikely that he will learn better ways of robbing, raping, or killing. That is not, of course, the intention of the authorities, who are interested in teaching him such things as skills and codes of conduct which will make him more likely to be-have acceptably when he leaves.

This is a particularly difficult assignment. The student who arrives at such a school has had unsatisfactory contacts with educational establishments. He has not learned much and has probably been told that it is his own fault. He is probably a dropout. That is one reason why he has not been able to fit into an acceptable way of life. The training school has an opportunity to bring about an important change, but how can it do so? What reasons can it give the young delinquent for acquiring some of the skills which will make nondelinquent behavior more likely?

In almost all our schools students study primarily to avoid the consequences of not studying, and the special power available to those who administer schools for delinquents favors the pattern. Students are generally coerced into studying. The by-products are familiar in school systems in general and are likely to be particularly conspicuous in a training school. The student will escape from the system if he can, he will vandalize it, and he will reject what he has learned in it as soon as the opportunity arises.

A New Learning Environment describes a different kind of social environment in a training school. It reports an experiment in "contingency management" under which students were given positive reasons for behaving well with respect to each other and for studying and learning. It was not easy to construct such an environment. Indeed the practical problems were often staggering. But solutions were found, in part with the help of the art which springs from a humane concern for people and in part through the application of a technology derived from a science of behavior. The result—the CASE project at the National Training School for Boys—may well take its place as a landmark in penal reform.

Preface

For more than two years we were involved in a special project with forty-one incarcerated teenage delinquents whose crimes ranged from auto theft and housebreaking to rape and homicide. Most of these youths had dropped out of public school and were equally unresponsive to the educational program within the federal penal system at the National Training School for Boys (NTS) in Washington, D.C.

Under grants from the Office of Juvenile Delinquency and Youth Development of the Department of Health, Education, and Welfare to the Institute for Behavioral Research, we and our associates designed and operated the CASE II-MODEL Project (Contingencies Applicable to Special Education—Motivationally Oriented Designs for an Ecology of Learning). The objective was the positive expansion of the academic and social repertoires of forty-one incarcerated adolescents through the use of operantly formulated contingency systems and the design of a special environment. By establishing an incentive plan, using rewards available in a free enterprise democracy (money and the things money can buy), we were able to increase the academic growth rate of these students two to four times the average for American public school students.

In a very real sense, those of us concerned with the analysis, education, and redirection of the behavior of these youths played a variety of roles, two of which were like those of Goldilocks and Alice

xix

in Wonderland. Like Goldilocks, we were trying to determine, by some rational method of testing and evaluation, exactly what was considered normal, just right—not too much behavior and not too little. Also, like Alice in Wonderland, we wanted these students to be aware of their own behaviors to assure that their performance was appropriate to the local environmental cues. We were not concerned merely with behavior itself but with a functional analysis of the ecology that maintained the behavior. For example, when a young man shouts at the top of his voice, jumps up and down, and waves his hand wildly, what is the message? Is this a Goldilocks or an Alice in Wonderland problem? Is this behavior exaggerated or is it inappropriate? The only way we can tell is by analyzing much more than the behavior itself. At a football game it is considered good school spirit, but in a public library it is deemed inappropriate. Also, the payoff for each type of behavior may differ. Behavior cannot be sensibly evaluated without analyzing its environment and considering its consequences.

Grossly inappropriate behaviors frequently bring young people social disapproval. Many who do not have effective psychiatric counseling through a good health insurance program end up in centers for delinquent youth. A large proportion of these youths are incompetent; they lack appropriate academic and social repertoires. Extreme poverty and incompetence and a high degree of inappropriate behavior bring the behaving youth into a mental hospital as a mental deviant or into a prison as a social deviant.

Some of the youths' behavior problems can be related to the inability of the schools to cope with, maintain, and educate them. Some analysts diagnose the high dropout rate and these learning problems as the result of our use of shoddy buildings and outdated teaching equipment in urban schools. Others find it useful to assess the student's IQ and to describe him as basically poor material to work with. Both reasons in various combinations have been used to explain the present disaster. The low IQ scores of poverty-pocket children have tended to reinforce those seeking supportive data for the viewpoint that these children should have special programs keyed to their present intellectual ability—vocational education or

Preface

a weakened academic curriculum. This particular attack has proven to be the most effective smoke screen for maintaining retarded teaching systems. It has permitted the politically supported and publicly financed school system to continue using inadequate learning environments (environments in the sense of ecologies rather than buildings and equipment).

In the penal system, this general viewpoint has been expounded and has been structured into a basic operating premise. Prison educational personnel tend to support nineteenth-century concepts of genetic limits as defined by intelligence tests, and they prepare remedial programs which separate these young people according to preconceived learning-potential categories. Low, dull, and dull normal students are respectively assigned to unskilled, semi-skilled, and educable categories. Those categorized as low and assigned to unskilled tasks are not permitted to use the educational facilities. The personnel assume that this group of young men is basically incompetent to perform in certain areas of human learning. They accept as supporting evidence that an eighteen year old with an IQ of 76—who is reading at fifth grade level and has not achieved competence in algebra, physics, and chemistry in the public school system—is incapable of learning. Instead, they assign him tasks which they consider appropriate to his ability, tasks that do not require reading and academic skills.

Although the existing system of education at the NTS selected only those who looked promising and gave them traditional public school programs, the CASE project population was assigned from all grade levels and dealt with every one of those students, even those who did not wish to participate in the project. We hypothesized that every inmate was student material, and we started our educational project with students selected for the project by a random procedure before their arrival.

Student participation in CASE II started on February 4, 1966, and continued for one full year. The project dealt with typical NTS juvenile offenders whose convictions were varied and who ranged from fourteen to eighteen years of age. One commonality for the entire group, whether they were black or white, from the hills of West Virginia, the streets of New York, the suburbs of New Orleans, or the farms of Tennessee, was that they were all school failures.

The goal of the CASE project was to increase the academic skills of all its students, no matter what their current behavior, and to prepare as many students as possible either to return to the public school system or to pass a high school equivalency exam. To fulfill this objective, the project designed a twenty-four hour learning environment, established new systems of operations, devised an economy based on academic achievement with scheduled reinforcement (which paid the students for competence), and hired the students to work for the CASE administration. The environment was planned to include choices and perquisites normally available to the average wage-earning American but not available to these youths in a prison. The students earned points (money) for academic performance and paid for their rooms, clothing, amusement, and gifts. They became, through their own educational achievement, working and paying members of the CASE society.

The general purpose of *A New Learning Environment* is to increase the reader's awareness of the effect a contingency oriented environment can have on human learning behaviors. The particular purpose is to indicate the effective use of behavioral control in the education of delinquent youth by describing a newly designed living structure, presenting specified procedures, and showing the results of objective tests and other behavioral measures. By including the systems and programs used throughout the project, with specific examples, we hope to encourage the reader to examine his own existing educational system in the light of specified behavioral objectives and measurement. We are convinced that the motivationally oriented environment would be of value not only to rehabilitation institutions (penal and mental) but also to the educational and psychological professions.

Strong indications that the principles employed in CASE II could be effective in the public school system are found in the increases—by as much as four grade levels—in academic skills as measured by nationally standardized tests, in positive attitudinal changes in the students, and in IQ as much as 27 points. Now, the principles and procedures described here are being employed by us and others of similar persuasion throughout the country in isolated programs within public schools. Problems in juvenile academic and social behavior continue to increase. Tomorrow, the shaping of appropriate behaviors and the redirection of those considered deviant will focus on those methods that have provided substantive behavioral change.

The completion of *A New Learning Environment* was prompted by many people. Although the final editorial work was done by us, credit must be given to the following people whose efforts made this book possible. Murray Sidman and Mary D. Cohen helped edit and synthesize the early 1400 page CASE II Report. John S. Bis, Joan E. Cohen, and Paul Larkin contributed to the CASE II Final Report. The authors gratefully acknowledge the contribution of Israel Goldiamond and Saleem Shah for their help in establishing specific program objectives, and of Herman Gewisgold and Robert Levinson for the valuable information they provided about the federal penal and probation system. The authors also are indebted to Myrl Alexander, director of the Federal Bureau of Prisons, Roy Gerard, superintendent of the National Training School for Boys, and Allan Childers, former superintendent of the National Training School for Boys, whose interest, encouragement and assistance helped make the CASE projects a reality. A special note of thanks must be given to those many visitors who came to CASE from other institutions and allied professions to vocalize their negative or skeptical judgments as well as their reinforcing comments. Having the project in Washington, D.C., made it a fish bowl and helped contribute to our success by forcing us to defend and explain our procedures to more than seven hundred vociferous visitors.

Washington, D.C. HAROLD L. COHEN
September 1971 JAMES FILIPCZAK

Contents

Foreword by R. Buckminster Fuller   xi

Foreword by B. F. Skinner   xvii

Preface   xix

1. To State the Case   1

2. Environmental Reinforcers   16

3. Design for Learning   37

4. General Operations   60

5. Cultural and Interpersonal Results   81

6. Academic Results   108

7. What Happened to the Students?   133

Appendix A: Comparison of Case II
and the National Training School
for Boys   144

Contents

Appendix B: The Student Educational
    Researcher's Handbook   152

References   185

Index   187

A New Learning Environment

A Case for Learning

Chapter 1

To State
the Case

*A*ll situations are potentially educational. A functional analysis of the behavior of the individual who is interacting with his environment enables us to distinguish between an environment that increases or maintains educational behaviors and one which does not. One term, *behavior,* is essential to description of the learning process.

In the process of evolution, the organism that continues to behave and survives because of his ability to differentiate his behaviors by environmental feedback (survival cues) is the organism that learns and therefore grows. An infant starts to learn the moment he is born. His early learning environments are extremely well controlled, protected, and ordered by the parent. Without such an ordered and controlled environment, the child would die. Health experiences—fulfillment of man's biological necessities and physical and intellectual growth—are programed by the adult world through the adult's accumulation of successful experiences. The child's contact with his world expands with the extension of his own developing senses. His first tactile sense of the world is expanded by his

1

senses of sound and smell, which carry him beyond his physical limitations—namely, the extension of his hand and the position of his mouth. His sense of hearing introduces additional stimuli which further cue him to his survival program—for example, the approaching steps and the voice of his mother act as a distant introduction to his eating and cuddling schedule. With the later development of his sense of sight, he increases the range of his cues and his differentiating experiences.

In order to learn, the child must make some response to this expanding series of cues. Because his response to cues has both gratifying and aversive consequences, he starts to be selective. He varies the strengths and the schedule (the time and place) of his own responses. He learns to discriminate and does not respond to all cues alike. In short, he starts to differentiate his responses and develops an expanding behavioral repertoire. The action of environmental stimuli upon individual behavior and the reaction to these stimuli (the student's response) produce a change in the individual. This change is called learning.

Both open and closed institutional systems deal with the individual in an environment designed to produce specified learning objectives. An attempt is made to examine the student's past behavioral record and to prescribe an interpersonal therapy program based on that behavior. In the CASE II-MODEL project (Contingencies Applicable to Special Education—Motivationally Oriented Designs for an Ecology of Learning) we planned rehabilitation by inculcating new academic and socially appropriate behaviors under a schedule of reinforcement, while extinguishing inappropriate, antisocial behaviors by a schedule which was either competing or nonreinforcing. The purpose of incorporating a set of specified academic content performances with a schedule of reinforcement was to program the individual for success. In the CASE program, we had adolescents who had had long histories of failure—both at home and in school. The punishing aspects of failure to perform in these environments produce not only school dropouts but dropouts from life. The normal educational environment is a rigged slot machine—on a limited hold and a variable schedule of little success, heavily sprinkled with performance schedules that lead to no payoff, failure. The standard educational environment is aversive and punishing to a student with a limited history of success and a small academic repertoire.

Those who are assigned to the role of rehabilitator often ignore the fact that the public schools control the bulk of the early child's and young adult's academic and social development. The student who arrives in class unprepared is anxious—that is, has a higher probability for failure. He hopes the teacher will not call on him to recite or to respond to a question. If the child is called upon and responds with an incorrect answer, he has a dilemma. He may be laughed at by his peers or be reprimanded by the teacher. In truth, he may have studied but was unable to understand the material because it was inappropriate for his level or was poorly written. For a teenager, going to class unprepared is like going to a swimming party even though he is inappropriately dressed or cannot swim. Such an experience—in which one cannot respond to the demands of the situation—is not gratifying.

The analogous classroom environment has been ungratifying and therefore aversive for a student whose history of performance has been poor. He drops farther and farther in his seat to avoid direct contact with the situation. Eventually he escapes the aversive environment by removing himself completely. He drops out of school.

The students in our project who had dropped out of school before being sentenced for their crimes had had little or no academic success. By pretesting them and assigning them programed instruction at a level at which they could perform successfully, we guaranteed success for each individual on whatever level he began. Little by little each student, through this step-by-step process, found that he was able to achieve 90 per cent accuracy or better in his test work. We did not lower the requirements of the academic work, just as we do not lower the requirements of life. Youngsters recognize the dropping of standards as "Mickey Mouse," as something

3

that is done for an individual with lower intelligence, for a second class citizen. A student already under racial or regional discrimination is angered further by an attempt to lower standards.

American society demands a completed high school education for industrial success and a college degree for administrative success. The young school dropout delinquent is aware of these requirements. Saying to him, "Well, you can't read very well so you won't get through high school, but why don't you get a job as a plumber's assistant or a laundry presser?" only reinforces his initial viewpoint—that he is not very bright and is considered a second class citizen. If it is good and necessary for the free, healthy, nondelinquent adolescent to complete school and be prepared for a new technological revolution, then it is necessary and good for the delinquent to have some of the same goals.

We did not produce an environment which increases academic skills and maintains these newly acquired behaviors just to demonstrate and prove a learning theory and to develop an educational technology. These newly acquired educational skills also reinstate in the young deviant the promise that he can be normal—that he can be successful in an area where he formerly was unsuccessful and that this success will enable him to reenter the mainstream of the American adolescent world—the public school system and the opportunities that follow.

It can be argued that it is unfair to tell a youngster with an IQ below 90 that he can learn to read and write and do algebra like the rest of the "healthy," socially adjusted adolescent group. After all, the school system has not been able to get this youngster to succeed, and his past academic performance provides evidence of his inability to pass. Why establish false hope? Isn't this a false contract?

To test these assumptions, we designed and operated a pilot project, CASE I, which dealt with sixteen students from the regular population of the National Training School for Boys in Washington, D.C. A half-day program was conducted from February 24, 1964, to October 31, 1965 (Cohen, Filipczak, and Bis, 1967). We tested the use of programed instructional material and explored the range and schedule of reinforcers needed to sustain a contingency managed

4

system. The results convinced us that a twenty-four hour environment would be useful as a next step, and CASE II followed. The completed work in both programs clearly demonstrates that not the youngster but the public school system and its ecology have failed. The youngster is not mentally bankrupt but the public school and the systems that sustain it are.

The design of the CASE II project, the use of new schedules of reinforcement in a contingency oriented environment, the use of programed instruction, and the design of a new curriculum increased competence in youngsters who recognize their new academic success in marked contrast with their previous failure.

The main aim of the project was to develop procedures which would establish and maintain educational behaviors in a penal setting. Continuous recording systems were used to measure the educational behaviors and to assess the efficacy of the procedures. Although the results described here were obtained with an institutionalized deviant population, we consider the procedures to be of greater generality. Stemming as they do from research in the experimental analysis of behavior and environmental design, these findings are consistent with a body of data currently being obtained, with various populations in other types of institutions using similar procedures. The institutions range in degree of custodial control from a mental hospital (Ayllon and Azrin, 1965) to a midwestern college (Cohen, 1964). The institutional populations range from psychotics (Goldiamond and Dyrud, 1968) and mental retardates (Sidman and Stoddard, 1966) to bright college freshmen (Cohen and Filipczak, 1968). The findings of the CASE II study are also consistent with the basic procedures used in laboratory research. Promising procedures are being developed to alter behavior in a programed manner (Lovaas, 1966). The procedures are also being extended to alter human behaviors of clinical relevance (Ferster, 1962). Moreover, an educational system in which student and system behaviors are continually monitored and measured may have general implications for educational systems which transcend the specific limitations of the present project.

The basic premise of CASE II was that educational behavior

is functionally related to its consequences and that—by setting up a situation in which appropriate consequences are made contingent upon changing behavioral requirements—these behaviors can be established, altered, maintained, and transferred. Although the setting was a penal institution, choice was maximized, and the limitations placed upon choice by arbitrary orders from authority were minimized. For example, students could, if they chose, rent a private room for sleeping, for which they paid the equivalent of eight dollars a week. Or they could choose to go on relief and sleep as boys do elsewhere in the National Training School, on bunk beds in an open area. Students could buy their own meals and order freely in a cafeteria, or they could choose to go on relief and eat standard institutional food served on metal trays. Students could buy their own clothing or wear prison issue; they could buy pictures and furnishings for their rooms and save for air transportation for a furlough home. They could pay an entry fee into a lounge and make purchases at a store.

A prison is a controlled welfare state in which the inmates are taken care of. We were told initially that this population consists of "con men and freeloaders" and that, given the choice of free lodging and food or earning better quality food, lodging, and clothing, they would choose to go on relief. This was simply not so. No student spent more than four weeks on relief during a fifty-two week period—and never more than two consecutive weeks.

In the past, the National Training School educational staff selected students whose ability to succeed had been predetermined and put them through standard classroom activity using standard texts and grading systems. Before the inception of the CASE II project, the bulk of the inmates at NTS were placed in shop programs of general maintenance, automotive repair, laundry, dishwashing, floor polishing, coal shoveling, and grounds keeping. That group was not permitted into the academic school. Approximately one half of the small group that did attend the academic school were considered—on the basis of increased Stanford Achievement Test scores—to be benefiting from school work. An even smaller group

6

was prepared to pass the tests for high school equivalency certification.

The goals of the CASE II project were to increase the academic behaviors of all of its students, no matter at what level they were, and to prepare as many students as possible within one year for return to the public school system.

CASE II students began living within the round-the-clock environment of Jefferson Hall, a converted dormitory building on the grounds of the National Training School, on February 4, 1966. These young men, aged fourteen to eighteen, had been convicted of homicide, general housebreaking, rape, armed robbery, and automobile thefts. Now they became Student Educational Researchers, hired to work for the CASE II administration. Students worked on programed courses and regular texts and attended programed classes and lecture classes. The product of their work for the CASE "corporation" was both intellectual wealth and personal buying power. Points (money) were earned through specified educational behaviors—studying for an hourly wage and passing tests at the required level of 90 per cent or better. They could choose to spend their points in many ways.

One reason we used points as the generalized reinforcer is quite obvious: money allows the student to engage in a variety of behaviors. A less obvious reason was that the opportunity to behave is one of the most powerful reinforcers known. Premack (1959) asserts that given two behaviors, one at a low probability and the other at a high probability, the more probable behavior can be used to reinforce the less probable if it is made contingent on it.

By providing money, we were making the more probable behavior which money can buy contingent upon less probable educational behavior. Eventually, through appropriate programing and environmental support, the educational behavior may come to be reinforced by nonmonetary rewards. But it is a principle of programing that we distinguish between our terminal requirement, or goal, and the current repertoire of the student whom we tie into. We may not wish him always to work for money, but we start with his value system—just as we begin with his level of knowledge and skills—and work from there.

Using money as a generalized reinforcer worked in our educational research environment, just as it does in our society. We all perform because there is something in it for us. When we study, the "something" may be a job or five dollars for each A. Today, for some college students, the grade of C or better is a means of staying out of Vietnam. Good grades enable some young people to hang around college and socialize and join fraternities. Some students see good grades as the way to get the degree which permits them to join their father's business or a large corporation. A car, marriage, children, or a trip to Europe are among other goals. Some of us even read and learn because we enjoy it, for the sheer pleasure of it. But America is not filled with people who find that knowledge is its own reward.

Although the American ideal is that everyone should perform at his best level and do well, our National Training School students demonstrated that they did not have such an ideal goal. So we used purchasing power as the extrinsic immediate reinforcer to get the academic behaviors started. Some young men are willing to wait for their delayed reinforcement, good report cards, diplomas, and so on, but our delinquent student-inmates wanted to know, "Man, what's the payoff *now?*" Like most of us, they were willing to work for money.

They earned their money-points (each point equaled one penny) by achieving academic success; their reinforcement was contingent upon performance. Their educational behavior was maintained by the total CASE II environment. In an ideal situation, the intrinsic consequences of a task itself maintain behavior. For example, one reads a novel to follow the development of the characters or plot or one reads in order to learn. However, we were dealing neither with ideal situations nor with students who had a history of such an approach to learning. Therefore, we developed a system of extrinsic reinforcements which were already strong in these students' repertoires and which lent themselves to being altered

8

gradually into the generally more desirable form of intrinsic reinforcement.

The points they received for correct answers to programed
or semiprogramed educational problems, tests, and other academic
performances could at any time be converted into material or social
reinforcers. They could rent and decorate a private room, order
clothes and other materials from a mail order catalog, or buy entrance into a recreational lounge, for example. They chose their own
rewards and did not have to convert their points into any specified
reinforcer; points could also be saved. By recording the points rather
than distributing them in money or token form, we avoided the
transference of negotiable points from one student to another. Points
could not be acquired in any way unrelated to the learning specified
by the CASE staff.

The academic program was voluntary and individualized.
The student-inmate did not have to do academic work. He worked
at his own pace on individualized curricula based on the results of
his pretesting. The only way he could earn sufficient points was to
study and complete the educational material recommended to him.
The variety of tests he took upon entering the project determined his
standing in various school subjects (he might score at a high school
level in mathematics and a third grade level in reading). After con-
sultation with an advisor, he was assigned programs which allowed
him to start work at the appropriate level for each subject. A grading system was developed which gave the student immediate access
to his own progress and the adequacy of his understanding. A grade
of at least 90 per cent or better was required on all programed
instruction. After he had completed a unit of study and had
achieved 90 per cent correct responses, the student was given an
exam through which he could earn additional points.

The model for the project was that of a student research
employee who checks in and out of the various activities for which
he is paid or for which he pays. As a Student Educational Researcher, the student was hired to do a job and paid to learn. The
immediate goal was to test the various programs, academic and

9

nonacademic. Whether he worked was up to him, but there were no free handouts.

An excerpt from the SER Handbook (see Appendix B) explains the student's role as a researcher:

Your title as a CASE II student is Student Educational Researcher *and as a researcher you will be paid for the work you do for CASE II. Your payment (salary) will be in points. These points can be used just as you would use money. You will be able to pay for a private room, buy your meals, buy clothing, use the lounge, and make purchases from the CASE store. Your position as a Student Educational Researcher will also enable you to take vacations from the National Training School and will hopefully provide you with those academic and social tools which will be available to you as a citizen of these United States. As a Student Educational Researcher you are a free citizen within the project. You will have choices in what you do, but your choices will also carry responsibilities.*

The new job started with the initial battery of entrance examinations, in which the students earned points for correct answers. This was more than an orientation to the system; it was an initial demonstration that the system did operate the way they were told it would. It also helped make the test results more valid. Nothing in the history of these boys had ever indicated to them that it might be to their advantage to do as well as possible on an academic test. Paying them for correct answers was a direct attempt to solve this problem. It is difficult to determine whether the points did, indeed, generate more valid test results than we would have obtained otherwise, for the tests themselves varied greatly in their predictive value. However, there were very few instances of a student's being started too low within an academic program as a result of his initial testing.

Each student was given a Handbook containing the rules and procedures of the project. Since many of the students were functionally illiterate, an oral examination based on the rule book was given shortly after it was issued. A score of 90 per cent or better on this examination earned points for the student and assured him of an individual study booth which served as his office.

To State the Case

The following excerpt from the Handbook explains its functions to the student.

It is the purpose of the Student Educational Researcher Handbook to provide an outline of your choices and responsibilities. This Handbook is for you to read when you start as a Student Educational Researcher and also to provide a reference for any future questions you may have. However, the Handbook is also a part of the CASE II learning process, and it will be changed as we all learn better ways of doing things. When changes are made you will always be notified. This Handbook is your very first job as Student Educational Researcher with CASE II. About one week from the time of your arrival into CASE II you will be given an orientation test which will tell us how well you understand the procedures of CASE II. You will be expected to pass this test with a grade of 90 per cent or better. But don't become too alarmed. The Handbook is only one part of the information and assistance you will be given during the orientation period. You will be interviewed by many of the staff and students and will have CASE II procedures fully explained and hopefully all of your questions answered before you are asked to take the orientation test.

The major behaviors for which points were given were the educational behaviors whose establishment and maintenance were the primary aims of the project. The students had so many academic deficiencies that a variety of options were available for programed material and classes they could take. A complete file of programs had been established, and it was possible for a student to progress from pre-arithmetic through geometry on programed material. There were also groups of study programs supplemented by classroom study and individual tutorials. Regular classroom teachers from the NTS academic school were employed in the project.

It was not necessary for students to complete large blocks of work or to wait long periods of time before earning points. Programs were subdivided into sections. The students were paid for successful completion of subsections and for taking examinations in which they demonstrated their mastery of the material.

A New Learning Environment

In addition to the central activity of earning points for academic work, CASE provided other supporting reinforcements. After all, money cannot do some very important things. For example, a young man playing basketball in front of his high school friends sets a difficult basket shot. The girl cheerleaders jump up and down, and the crowd cheers. Money cannot buy that kind of reinforcement, which adolescents refer to as goodness. This goodness comes out of a specific singular performance in an environment in which successful behavior is immediately reinforced by the peer group.

Group reinforcements are extremely powerful, and we attempted to program some of these into the system. For example, when a student did especially well on an exam (earned a grade of 100 per cent) the staff brought the accomplishment to the attention of the other students and commended him genially—"Gosh, that was great," or "Man, that's cool." Such a reward was recognition for a task performed. However, only a task that required some competent behavior or a large effort won such recognition. The student knew the difference between a task that required lots of competent behavior and one that was "Mickey Mouse."

The normal academic community has failed to use group reinforcement constructively. Athletic coaches have used it successfully, maintaining behavior and generating a tremendous amount of activity. Coaches reward any bit of advancement—they know that a pat on the back for a close try is reinforcing. Why is the athlete always running around a track, practicing every day and trying to better his score? His reward is that one big moment—the big payoff—when he runs in the track meet and succeeds and everybody cheers. Academic teaching staffs still rely primarily on long-range goals for all students.

CASE II also provided group reinforcement by allowing correctional officers to award points as bonuses for exemplary student behavior. This opportunity was a distinct change in the officer's role. In conventional institutions, he uses aversive control over social behavior. In CASE, the officer's relationship to the student was enhanced by his ability to award points, and several officers experienced great pleasure—and relief—at being able to assume a

12

positive rather than a threatening role. This was not a universal reaction. The usual conception of the correctional officer's job guarantees that a certain number of punitively oriented people will gravitate to it. Because all bonuses had to be recorded in the students' bankbooks and in the officers' records, it was possible for the CASE staff to examine what student behavior an officer considered constructive. It became evident that one officer was particularly reinforcing to those students who consistently made their beds or straightened their rooms. Another officer rewarded good language. One officer was noted to be concentrating bonuses on a particular student, and an investigation led to the discovery of a mutually exploitive relationship between officer and student. The officers had the opportunity to earn extra pay by attending special seminars at which they could learn constructive reinforcement techniques and could propose new programs of their own design.

Because the bonus system was successful with the officers, it was made available for all the other staff members, thereby providing a certain degree of flexibility in the management of problems that were unique to a particular student. For example, the data clerk noticed that one student had never received any fines in the educational area and recommended a special bonus for his good record.

Still other forms of reinforcement were provided by the carefully designed and controlled living conditions of the students. These young men were involved in the CASE II program twenty-four hours a day and most of their institutional activities were confined within the project. Environmental controls and behavioral procedures were developed to ensure that the students' requirements for rest, nourishment, hygiene, and recreation were met. In our encapsulated community they slept, ate, worked, studied, were guarded, had visitors, played, and were prepared for home furloughs. Their activities were constantly recorded and monitored; they punched timecards in and out of their hotel (sleep) area, the educational area, the testing room, and the lounge.

Specific environmental cues (facilities and signs) helped the student to differentiate his own behaviors. In CASE I, learning to

13

do math and respond to programed instruction started first in the classroom area and was extended into the library and the students' private offices. In CASE II, after a history of success in the educational area, the student took material into his private bedroom. This room was designed to sustain privacy; it also gave the student a piece of personal property which permitted him to invite friends in. It gave him an area where he gathered and displayed the results of his educational accomplishments—the things that he earned and that he purchased for his room. He was free to decorate it in any way he wished.

In his own room the student chose his activities—writing letters, drawing pictures, making models, or doing additional school work. The environment provided many physical stimuli. That one little room said, "Sleep," "Dress," "Man, bring your friends in," "Smoke," "Hang up your coat," "Let's talk about the outside world," "Let's eat some peanuts," "Write a letter to your girl friend." These behaviors were supported by the rules of the establishment and were permitted by the physical equipment and space design of the room. In his room the student could choose to sleep or to sit up all night and read. The rules, a private lamp, bed, and chair, plus his ability to read, made that behavior possible.

Special areas were scheduled for specified behavior. The student offices upstairs in the educational environment were used solely for the support of assigned academic tasks. The private office was provided because, at the beginning, space and instructional cues were critical reinforcers in the learning chain.

Some young people do their homework on the kitchen table and very often have to interrupt their studying so that the family can eat dinner. Some youngsters do their school work in bathrooms. Once a strong history of performance of a particular skill is established (for example, a long history of reinforcement for academic behaviors in an office), an individual can carry that behavior to any other environment which can physically sustain it. A learned behavior, although shaped in one particular environment, does not remain the "victim" of that original environment if the system of reinforcement was generalized.

To State the Case

The controls and reinforcements built into the students' private offices and bedrooms exemplify the total environmental approach which CASE II developed. This new living-learning structure, never before available in a federal prison, required changes in the behavior of correctional officers, teachers, and other members of the penal system. The altered behavior of staff had a marked effect upon the attitudes of students toward each other, the staff, and visitors. Another major result of this contingency management system was a sharp increase in academic skills as measured by national tests. The students' own success became a major source of reinforcement. Violent social behavior lessened to a surprisingly high degree despite the decrease in traditional punishment—for example, lockup, isolation, reduction of calorie intake—as a means of control. Consistent with a sharp increase in their scores on a Revised Army Beta test, the students accepted more responsibility for self-control. All the eight students who took the Tests of General Educational Development passed and received a high school equivalency certificate.

Environmental Reinforcers

As we have said, points were not the only reinforcing consequences available to the students, nor was academic learning the only kind of behavior reinforced. The various services and activities for which points could be spent not only maintained the reinforcing effectiveness of the points but made it possible for the students to acquire possessions, skills, and prestige which, in turn, opened up new opportunities for continuing development.

At first the students used the points to purchase soft drinks, milk, potato chips, Polaroid snapshots, entrance to and time in the lounge, entrance to and time in the library, smoke breaks, rental of a private room, rental of books and magazines, purchase of additional classroom time, private tutoring, and material from the outside world through mail order catalogs. From the catalog the student was able to purchase articles such as sports jackets, white shirts, ties, pants, Mother's Day cards, candy, flowers, and other desired items.

In addition to these primarily material reinforcements, students were able to earn some powerful nonmonetary rewards. Respect, approval by one's peers, and correctness help maintain human behavior in social groups, whether inside a prison or in a free society. Although our society is run on a powerful generalized reinforcer—money—we are also motivated to do good work, work we like, work we do well and/or work recognized by others, and work which brings us in contact with people we like. In a free society it is a social and judicial right to be with people we love, like, or respect. It is difficult for a young adult to learn how to obtain some of this form of reinforcement, that is, praise in educational areas, when he has little or none of the repertoire required to achieve competence and success in these educational and socially accepted areas. The CASE project used teaching machines, programed special classes, devised new testing methods, and planned a supportive environment based upon the generalized reinforcer of points, enabling most of the students to enjoy the reinforcement that comes from the excitement of being right 90 to 100 per cent of the time. The students also experienced approval for good work, not just from the CASE staff, but from the other students.

HOME FLOOR

The ground floor of Jefferson Hall was designed as the home floor. This provided a large number of potential reinforcing consequences for the students and was a critical area in the development of social skills and the kinds of behavior we characterize as personal pride, self-reliance, and individualism.

Sleeping quarters were established on the home floor. A series of individual rooms insured a modicum of rented privacy for each student who wanted it and could afford it. The private rooms were designed to be home bases for the CASE students, where they slept, studied, and relaxed. The weekly rental for these rooms started at six hundred points (inflation eventually increasing this cost to eight hundred points). A special discount was available if a student rented the same room for four consecutive weeks; the rental for the fifth week was two hundred points.

At the beginning the rooms were sparsely furnished and impersonal. Each was equipped with a bed, a chair, and a lockable storage-desk unit. The door swung down to form a desk/writing surface. Indications of pride in ownership developed rapidly. The students decorated their rooms with items purchased in the store (pillows, pictures, model planes, and so on), drawings and items from their classes, and personal photographs. Illustrations ranged from Rembrandt's "Son" to *Playboy* centerfolds.

Private shower stalls were rented on a weekly basis at a rate of two hundred points. Students who rented these could shower at any time until midnight each evening. This wide latitude in time helped eliminate social problems that can come from the interaction of nude boys. When their earnings enabled them to do so, the students chose to rent the shower. A general shower room was given free as part of the weekly room payment.

A coin operated commercial washer enabled the students to wash the clothing they had purchased. The rate was twenty-five points per load. Students often pooled their soiled clothing to make a load for the machine, and alternated payment. The project store had a stock of detergents, bleaches, and other laundry items for student purchase. In addition to maintaining their purchased clothing, some of the students used equipment available on the home floor to launder and press the uniforms provided by NTS. They purchased a washing machine rental slip in the store and deposited it with the home floor officer who kept a supply of coins to activate the machine. Clothes were delivered to the cleaners and gifts were wrapped and taken to the post office for the students at no cost beyond the cleaning charge or mailing costs.

Students who were either unwilling or unable to pay for both their room and board went on relief. This meant that they moved from their private rooms and, with a minimum of personal belongings, moved into an open area in front of the officer's station on the home floor where two double bunks were placed. In addition to their loss of privacy, relief students were required to wear the NTS issue khaki clothing, place all personal belongings (with the exception of basic toilet articles) in storage, and eat standard NTS meals from a metal tray. Students on relief were awakened by the correctional officer each morning and required to make their bunks, clean the area around their bunks, wash themselves and shave. Each evening they had to be in their relief bunk at lights out. They were not permitted to visit with other students in their private rooms nor to have any Sunday visitors except their immediate family, whom they saw in the entrance hallway rather than in the lounge. Relief status in CASE was equivalent to standard prison living conditions at NTS.

The distaste for relief status was evident. Two students who were financially stable voluntarily chose to go on relief but requested a return to their private rooms and the associated privileges after only two days. The withdrawal of privacy and privileged participation was avoided whenever possible. Given a choice, students worked on the educational floor and/or on a part-time job to maintain themselves and their private rooms.

Project data show that the students spent slightly over 40 per cent of their total available leisure time on the home floor. Aside from routine activities such as laundering or ironing, the students met with friends in their own rooms, listened to the radio, or watched television on rented or privately purchased sets. They wrote letters or read, talked with the home floor officer, decorated their rooms, constructed models, and attended to their personal hygiene.

STORE AND LOUNGE

The CASE II store, containing a sales center and lounge on the first floor, was designed as a place where the students could translate points into specific indications of personal preference. The store provided a showcase of items for rental or purchase; each was selected to whet the appetite of the buyer, to provide incentive to the consumer, and to increase opportunities for decision making. One student invested in a large wardrobe of clothes, another spent most of his points on games of pool, and a third saved toward his pending release.

In its twofold function as the base for the sales center and the lounge, the store handled all sales to students and maintained data related to purchases. All purchases, food, room rentals, clothing, and so on, were made through a bookkeeping system. No points as such exchanged hands. All bookkeeping was done after 9:00 P.M. so that the banking and ledger sheet could be available for morning posting and a new day's purchasing activity could begin. The variety of items was displayed attractively to encourage purchases. Lists were visually organized to encourage use of available services. Also, mail order and chain store catalogs were readily available to provide a large selection beyond the scope of physical space for stock displays.

When the number of brand names available to the CASE students was expanded, a by-product was observed: the students became discriminating shoppers. The storekeeper was told that certain brands of spray starch stuck to the irons, or that a better product had been purchased by some student on a shopping trip. Newspapers were scanned for sales, and point conscious students requested specific items based on their earnings. The frequent changing of regular stock reflected the current needs of the project population. For instance, the introduction of the washing machine necessitated a supply of laundry products. Similarly, the purchase of transistor radios by several students necessitated availability of replacement batteries.

The lounge was the locus of student recreational activities. The students were able to gather there and relax following the day's school work, outdoor sports activities, or evening employment. The majority of the project's recreational equipment was located here. As a site of casual recreation, the lounge had a set of cues appropriate to its function. The entire setting implied relaxation: comfortable chairs, tables with newspapers and magazines, racks containing paperback books, card tables, a television set. At the store counter, the students could request use of the pool table, jukebox, pinball and bowling machines, slot car track and equipment, ping-pong table, or soda from the dispenser in the lounge. The lounge was the place to go for diversion, such as playing games, dancing, or enjoying the company of friends. Families were greeted in the lounge when they came to visit and were invited to use the equipment if their student-host paid the required fees.

Environmental Reinforcers

Use of the lounge facility required payment of an entrance fee. The price varied from one hundred points per hour at 3:00 P.M. to 4:00 P.M. on weekdays, to zero points during visiting hours on Sundays. (See page 180 for lounge hours and costs.) Experimentation during the original CASE I project had demonstrated that competition between the lounge and the educational activities was a direct function of the lounge entrance fee. The more it cost them, the less likely the students were to prefer the lounge. This is the reason both for the limited availability of the lounge and for its greater cost during hours when its use might have conflicted with the educational program. However, the students still had considerable freedom in this respect. The basic choices they had were to earn points, to spend them in leisure activities, or to spend them for material, social, and educational gain. The proportion of their income which the students spent in each of these ways is an important measure of the effectiveness of the project.

The lounge also provided a door-sales service, designed so that students of marginal wealth could avoid the lounge entrance fee when they only wanted a small item. Door sales included any item which could be taken to the home floor, excluding soft drinks, which were not permitted there for sanitary reasons.

Students were charged for the items purchased through mail order catalog and newspaper sales at the time of their delivery. A student rarely failed to budget for a purchase, and catalog items were never returned for lack of funds. On one occasion when a student found the item he had purchased was too small for him, another student asked to purchase the item and a new order in a larger size was placed for the original purchaser. A total of 188,371 points was spent in catalog sales.

Student sales were permitted when a student wanted to dispose of some of his goods for "cash," a kind of pawning procedure. A student could take an item he wanted to sell to the store, along with an interested buyer, or he could display in the store an item he wished to sell. The storekeeper transacted the sale. The seller received the amount (minus a 5 per cent service charge) as addition to the balance on his store card, and the buyer paid the purchase price.

In addition to the items the students could rent in the lounge, the store offered other equipment for rental: tape recorders (used by members of the CASE student newspaper staff), typewriters (used by individuals to write both personal and formal letters for outside-the-project delivery and by the newspaper staff for composition of the newspaper), portable phonographs (used by individual students to play their personally-purchased records both in the lounge and on the home floor), extra lamps (to provide additional lighting in the private rooms), and the laundry equipment.

Buddy purchases were allowed if a student wanted to treat a friend to store purchases or services and the friend could pay his own lounge entrance. One student could buy a round of sodas for his friends one day, and another in the group would pick up the tab the next day. A television room, with space for twenty students, was separate from the lounge: There students could unwind before returning to the home floor. Although it was difficult for the store-keeper to observe the activities of the students in the television room and students did attempt escape from this room, it was felt that the risks were justified by the privileges this room afforded the students. Entry was permitted after payment of normal lounge rates.

FOOD SERVICE

Each new student was given three to five days of free room and board when he entered CASE—the days between his entrance and the beginning of a new room/meal week. After this initial period, the food service became an integral part of the contingency system. This was a radical departure from usual institutional practice. Students did not have to work to eat, but they did have to earn points if they wanted to eat better food than the ordinary institutional fare and to do so under pleasant circumstances. As in all institutions—armed services, universities, hospitals, and so on—the food service was a focal point for many of the students' expressions of both dissatisfaction and satisfaction. The system had to be monitored carefully and revised as problems arose. It was a critical area, both in its own right and as a powerful prop for the effectiveness of the points and for the maintenance of point-producing behavior.

During the first five months of the project, students could select a meal from three basic plans: Plan A (cost, nine hundred points per week) featuring the best choice, quantity, and quality of food; Plan B (cost, six hundred points per week) with limited choice and quantity; and relief, a basic sustenance for students who could not pay for meals. Both Plan A and Plan B were fancier than those provided in a traditional penal institution. Menus were posted on the home floor, and each Thursday evening the students completed a room/meal request form indicating which meal plan they desired (and could afford) for the following week. Students on relief could not use the china plates, cups and saucers, or cutlery of the normal dinnerware. Their meals were served on metal trays with metal cups and spoons.

Several problems led to the abandonment of this first meal system. First, the staff of the hired catering service did not keep dependable working hours and were unable to deal civilly with the students (whom they viewed as criminals). Therefore, an experimental project staff member was reassigned as chef.

Second, the students themselves offered certain valid objections to the system. They felt that they did not have optimum choice in meal planning because they were forced to make weekly selections. Also, they were not consuming all of the food to which they were entitled. Both the students and staff felt that the quality of food had decreased inordinately during the first five months. Student reactions included, "He (the food service director) invents foods," and the extreme, "New food won't help a bad cook." The staff realized that an open cafeteria would be closer to the real world and would increase the students' opportunities for making decisions. It would also give the staff an opportunity to manipulate prices (to lower prices on foods that were less desirable to students) and expand the palate of the students.

Therefore, a totally open food service plan was instituted. Students deposited one thousand points in lieu of signing up for a preferred meal plan. They could then purchase anything that was available from the food service and were charged individually for each item. If the student spent more than the deposit, he was charged additional points at the end of the week. If he did not spend the one thousand point deposit, the remainder was credited on his subsequent payroll form. The student could choose whatever suited his taste and point account. A fancy, full dinner meal (comparable to Plan A under the previous system) would cost the student between sixty-five and one hundred points. It was possible under this system to charge more for items in great demand and less for items that teenagers do not normally prefer—thereby directing choice. It was also possible to clear the icebox by charging extremely low prices for bargain leftovers. Students on relief were given a nutritious meal drawn from the basic food provisions.

The food service director made a point of insuring—particularly on holidays—that the students had the finest possible meals, and he always set a visually pleasing table. During one holiday period he expended considerable effort preparing a sumptuous tray of hors d'oeuvres and the students working in the kitchen noticed his extra work. When none of the students ate the hors d'oeuvres, the staff became curious. When they asked about it, they were startled to hear one student say, "We aren't going to eat those things. We know how hard Mr. Hamilton worked on them, and we wouldn't spoil his pretty plate for anything." The food service director had become a consistent favorite of the students.

There were some notable side benefits of the open cafeteria system: First, the staff was able to buy meals on the site of the project. This was of great benefit to the project because, during lunch particularly, there were sufficient female staff available to provide the students with feminine models for proper etiquette. The students were very aware of the presence of women during these meals and generally endeavored to conduct themselves in a proper manner. Certain students became indignant if off-color words were spoken and tried to insulate the women from any offensive remarks. Second, the presence of staff, both male and female, throughout all meals was found to be of general value. Many of the students took the opportunity to discuss their particular problems quite openly and frankly with staff members. Third, the project provided part-time cafeteria jobs for students who qualified. This provided some students with basic food-service training that was useful after they were released from the NTS.

BANKING SYSTEM

Rules for the CASE bank were based upon standard banking regulations. A savings account could be opened for one thousand points with interest rates comparable to current commercial rates. Procedures simulated those of a bank yet allowed the student to exercise complete control over his finances. (Procedures are on page 155.) Some exceptions to standard operation were made to facilitate the operation of the store (in which the bank was located). For instance, the minimum of one thousand points required to open an account (later reduced to five hundred points) discouraged students from using it as a petty cash repository. Similarly, the fee for withdrawals discouraged the swinging door approach to savings. Bank days were selected to minimize the problems of the payday rush, and bank hours were established during a relatively quiet sales period. Upon student suggestion, bank days were extended to Friday; many students claimed they could not hold their points over the weekend for Monday deposit, and this concurrent-with-payday deposit allowed them to save before willpower deserted them. Seven days' notice on withdrawals of cash was necessary to provide time for obtaining sufficient petty cash funds to cover the withdrawals. Such withdrawals were for town trips, shopping trips, and furloughs, the only times when points were converted to cash for student use. A total of 286,740 points ($2,867.40) were deposited by twenty-eight students between April 5, 1966 and February 2, 1967. Single deposits ranged from five hundred to nineteen thousand points and individual balances ranged from five hundred to twenty thousand points.

An entering student was permitted to take out an orientation loan. The amount of the loan was sufficient to permit him to pay for his room and meals (beyond the first few free ones) and have an excess for personal purchases until his first full pay period's earnings were accumulated. Loans were repaid at two hundred points per week with a charge of 1 per cent per week on the unpaid balance. From the very beginning the student was on his own, earning his way. Interest-free loans were permitted for enrollment in special classes and were initiated to encourage the students to take classes. A lengthy repayment period also encouraged students to apply for such loans.

A student could request funds to tide him over a critical period. For example, if the student's family wanted to visit during a weekend, and the student did not have sufficient funds to entertain them, he could borrow. If a student had difficulty with an academic program so that his earnings were inadequate to pay for a scheduled movie, his debts were examined to discern his previous pattern of earning. If the student had been sitting out his days on the educational floor making no effort to complete material, he was told that he was a poor loan risk and a loan was refused. Emergency loans were made for less than one thousand points and had to be repaid in total at the next pay period.

Loans were not granted for trips. Normally, the student had to have repaid his orientation loan by the time he was eligible for travel. However, certain circumstances mitigated against rigid adherence to stipulated regulations. When major illness or death occurred in the student's family, the NTS allowed him to take an emergency leave. A total of five emergency leaves were taken by three CASE students. One student was permitted to visit his mother at home during a period of crisis in her illness and later attended her funeral. Another student visited his mother twice while she was confined in Walter Reed Army Medical Center in Washington, D.C., for exploratory surgery. The fifth trip was permitted for a student to attend the funeral of his stepfather in Washington, D.C. None of these students were eligible, under strict interpretation of the regulations, to make project-approved trips. The first student mentioned did not have funds sufficient to cover the cost of the trip to visit his mother and was granted $135.00 from the NTS chaplain's fund. He subsequently repaid the chaplain at the rate of $10.00

26

per week from funds earned in the project. All other emergency leaves were paid for with funds earned by the students.

The project provided six different means for the student to contact his family and friends: letters, phone calls, in-project visits, escorted individual trips, town trips, and furloughs. Specific student behavioral requirements were established for each of these except letter writing and in-project visits, and specific staff members were responsible for supervising each of these programs.

Anyone whose name appeared on the approved visitor correspondent list could visit a student in the CASE project. Sunday was set aside as the normal visiting day, but the families of out-of-town students were allowed to visit during the normal hours of student movement in the building. All visitors were guests of the project students. The student paid for all meals, refreshments, and entertainment for his visitors. All items were paid for at the time of purchase, except meals, which were paid for prior to the visit. Sunday visitors were limited to a three hour period, from 1:00 to 4:00 P.M. Visiting hours were arranged individually for weekday visitors so that a student could apply for a sightseeing trip with his family—leaving around 10:00 A.M., returning with the family for 5:00 P.M. dinner, and entertaining them in the lounge until 8:00 P.M.

Because all transactions within the project were made with points, visitors were not permitted to purchase items for CASE students. Consequently, the student who was short of points could visit with his family, but he could not entertain them as well as the students who had sufficient points. After May 16, students were required to pay a ten point fee for lounge use during the Sunday visiting hours. This change was effected to defray costs incurred for lounge cleanup after the visiting hours. No appreciable decrease in lounge attendance was recorded.

The student could buy dinner for his family within the project. If he desired to do so, he was required to inform the food service personnel by signing a weekly list and noting the number of

27

guests that he planned to have. This registration was to be completed by Friday evening to insure that the food service could plan for the meals needed. Again, points were the only means of exchange, and the visitors could not pay for these meals. To provide a degree of privacy and ease, visitors' meals were served at the beginning and at the end of the normal Sunday dinner hour and their tables were decorated.

To make a phone call, a student was required to submit a written request form by 8:00 A.M. on the date he desired to place the call. This form was then reviewed by a member of the data staff. Students were allowed to initiate phone calls after two weeks' residence in the project if they had received no major fines (one hundred points or more) or disciplinary action during the previous two-week period. The student paid for the call on an established area distance/scale (see page 171). Students could make five distinct types of trips, based upon their length of stay in the project and their educational and social behavior. These are described on pages 164 and 166.

Like the food service, the family-contact plans deprived no student of any right he would have had if he were not in the project. But, by making the more desirable alternatives contingent on earning points, another strong prop was added to the educational programs through which the students earned points. Contrary to what might be supposed, these boys were not alienated from their families despite the often deplorable physical and social environments in which they subsisted. Family contact was a vital requirement for most of the students, and some of their most disastrous behavioral breakdowns were directly traceable to attempts at communication which the families did not reciprocate. Opportunities to demonstrate both educational and material acquisitions to their families were a major source of gratification to the students, as was social status within the project.

PROGRAMS FOR LEISURE TIME

During the students' leisure hours, special programs were available for which they paid an entrance fee. These were more formalized activities than those provided by the lounge and outdoor recreation. The library, sports classes, and movies were available to all students except those who were on relief or on restriction.

The library was a locus for leisure reading and quiet activity. In addition to books purchased by the project, twelve magazine and two newspaper subscriptions, the Washington, D.C. Public Library bookmobile deposited and exchanged approximately one hundred books with the library each month. Except on Sunday, students were charged fees for any entrance into the library, even if they only wanted to pick up a book. This was done to encourage those students who came to the library to take advantage of the full time allowed per entrance fee. Once a student had paid his entrance fee, he could leave the library, do anything he desired for a period of time, and return to complete the time he had paid for. With the above procedures in effect, the librarian never had disturbances in the library and never found books or other library articles defaced.

The librarian requested permission to award bonuses for written reports on books and articles read in the library. He established performance standards and awarded free passes to the library and to the Saturday night movies as payoff for successful written reports. This last procedure maintained the interest and participation of the students who already used the library but did not attract new students.

Feature length recreational films were selected by the student government and shown in the large classroom on the second floor of Jefferson Hall. The most regular film program was called the "CASE II Saturday Night Movie" and included such notable films as *Caine Mutiny, Arsenic and Old Lace, Fail-Safe, The Bridge on the River Kwai,* and *How Green Was My Valley,* while not disregarding such topical considerations as *Twist Around the Clock, Gidget Goes Hawaiian,* and *The Master American Counterfeiters.* Animated comedies and other short subjects were also provided with each major film. The storekeeper advertised the movies, sold tickets, and sold confections between movie reels. On project holidays, daytime movies were shown by the storekeeper in the lounge. The sale of movie tickets never proved financially profitable to the project; the number of students attending never exceeded 75 per cent of the population. But the diversion the films afforded the students made these offerings worthwhile in the context of the total project operations.

Sports classes in weightlifting, wrestling, and tumbling were offered during the evening. These gave the students one more area of free choice for spending their points. Entrance fee for each sports class was two hundred points. In addition, free outdoor sports activities were available for students in good standing. In front of Jefferson Hall were a baseball diamond, an outdoor basketball court, and horseshoe pits. Jefferson Hall also had a large front porch which permitted lounging during warm weather.

The students voted to have student barbers from the NTS barbering program come to Jefferson Hall on Saturdays. In return, the student barbers were to receive one dollar per hair cut. At the beginning of the program, the students paid half and the project subsidized the other half. Later, the students paid seventy-five cents and the project paid twenty-five cents. A list of students purchasing haircuts was made up by the home floor correctional officer. This list was passed to the storekeeper, who deducted the appropriate amount from each student's card. NTS student barbers were happy to get the CASE job assignment because it gave them cash with which to purchase their own set of barbering tools upon certification of their course work.

SCHOOL RELEASE PROGRAM

A school release program was instituted for students whose academic and social progress indicated that they were ready for placement in the public school system. Four students took part in this program. The school release students were given scholarships which paid for their room costs and meal charges up to the amount of one thousand points. In addition, they were able to earn points in the project to provide themselves with bus fare, school lunches, and clothing.

Students in this program were paid for the amount of time

30

they spent in evening study on the educational floor as well as for work completed. If they wished to completed programed instruction, they were paid the standard rate. A standard amount of cash was made available to the students from their earnings for lunch and bus fare. Any exceptions to the normal funds had to be requested through data control and banking and cleared by the Committee for Student Affairs. For example, funds for gym equipment were approved; a request for a large sum to be spent at a school dance was not.

CASE JOBS

Four types of job skill training programs were available within the project: office clerk and assistant, kitchen assistant, fry cook, and janitorial and maintenance. Students who wanted to supplement their income from educational work could apply for an available position. Although these programs were all in force throughout the project, no formalized written training curriculum was developed nor were written instructional materials used. Both part-time (after school) and half-day work schedules were developed for these student workers. Pay was proportional to the complexity of the job. The janitorial job became popular on a short range basis; typically, students who were having difficulty with educational programs would request the position and keep it only until they were able to sustain themselves on their educational income.

Educational prerequisites were often defined to insure a minimum level of worker competence; concurrent educational achievement was required, and provisions for dismissal were outlined. In general, the project emphasized academic rather than job training. This was done not because job training was considered unnecessary, but because time, staff, and financial support were not available for both. The decision to concentrate on academic training was based on two major considerations. First, the glaring lack of skill the students demonstrated in such basic academic areas as reading, writing, arithmetic, and speech would have prevented the students from obtaining even the most menial jobs. These de-

31

ficiencies had to be overcome if the students were to have choices available which would permit them to break out of the self-defeating cycle of their normal outside environment.

Second, the project staff were convinced that these students were able to acquire the same kind of education that our society normally expects of its youth. There was a deliberate rejection of any attempt to prepare these students for the kind of jobs for which some of even the most progressive social planners consider them fit. The aim, instead, was to provide them with the kinds of behavior that would permit them to enter the mainstream of the educational process. High expectations were set; high standards of performance were required; contingencies were designed to generate something more than minimal behavioral adaptation to the demands of society.

FINES AND BONUSES

One of the most detailed methods for measuring and modifying social behaviors involved the use of fines and bonuses which staff members authorized as a consequence of student behavior. This system provided rewards and punishment that were recordable with respect to time, place, behavior, and degree, on a scale readily understandable by both students and staff members. Problem solving could be shifted from a basis of exaggerated expressions of hostility, rejection, and the like, to a basis of rationally understandable consequences.

When a student engaged in behaviors that appeared to warrant some punitive action, the first recourse chosen by the staff member who witnessed it was usually to issue a fine. The fine was to be consistent with the severity of the infraction. If the deduction of the fine resulted in a deficit on the student store card, the student was not permitted to make purchases. However, no additional fine resulted for overspending because project procedures would thereby produce a system of double loss. Within an eight-month period, there were about three times as many bonuses as fines: 1245 bonuses as opposed to 411 fines. The frequency of bonuses was about 156 per month and frequency of fines was about 51 fines per month.

It was found that an effective punishing consequence for

improper behavior during the week was to refuse the student the privilege of attending the lounge during visiting hours. This privilege withdrawal produced no detrimental incidents during visiting hours. Students always conducted themselves with decorum.

Students were considered absent without official leave if they were one hour late in returning from an approved trip or if they at any time absented themselves from the grounds of the NTS without approval. If the student returned to the project, the following conditions were effected: He was placed on probation for one month. If he did not conduct himself in a satisfactory manner during this period of probation, he could be remanded to the custody of the NTS. He was placed on room restriction for at least five working days, commencing the day following his return to Jefferson Hall. During the one month probationary period, all mail and visiting privileges were restricted to contact with his immediate family. All points accumulated in his bank account and on his store card were confiscated by the project. They were to be returned on a specified schedule. Any "good time" earned through proper compliance with Federal Bureau of Prisons regulations could be withheld, depending on the severity of the case. He was considered a newly entering student and all residency time accrued and prerequisites fulfilled were obviated. Private study office privileges were suspended if the student had incurred any charges (such as correctional officer time spent to return the student to the project) from this AWOL, and the suspension remained in effect until such time as the charges were paid. The student was not permitted to choose a relief status until all debts were paid to insure that maximum effort was expended within the program. All final and special conditions were to be specified by a full meeting of the Committee on Student Affairs, with the student present. During the term of the project, and due principally to the relaxation of traditional custodial surveillance, nine students were absent without leave. In addition, three students overstayed leaves.

STUDENT GOVERNMENT

A student government, or student-elected body, operated for five months but was eventually dissolved by vote of the whole student body. The students eventually realized that on matters of consequence to them, they could appeal directly to the project staff, thus short-circuiting the student government. The student government was born out of the following event.

At the initiation of the project the director arbitrarily assigned a very high price to the pool table—150 points per half hour. In less than a week's time a few students gathered around the director mumbling and grumbling, saying that the price was too high. During that first encounter, one student said, "Man, we don't pay that much in the District." The director pointed out that he had no knowledge of the price structure in the District or anywhere else. Two students said they would call the local pool halls in the District of Coumbia, Maryland, and Virginia and determine the price. In fact, they argued that they should take the prices from these three communities, add them up, divide by three, and that should be the price for pool per hour. It was agreed that the Committee for Student Affairs (composed of the director, associate director, assistant director for data control and banking, educational director, and the chief correctional officer) would accept the new price structure if the students would follow through with their recommended plan.

The visibility of the success of the students' interaction with the ruling powers of the program was clear, and the students indirectly petitioned to create a government. The Committee for Student Affairs approved the establishment of a student government with one reservation—that the students take a seminar from the young librarian, who was also a law student, on how to form a government, and thereby become knowledgeable about parliamentary procedures and Robert's Rules of Order.

When the student government was finally formed and elections were held, the president and vice president were invited to join the Committee for Student Affairs as voting members, each carrying half a vote. The officers of the student government participated in the making of rules and in evaluation of infractions of the laws of CASE. They became the vehicle for the expression of the students' viewpoints to the Committee as well as the Committee's viewpoint back to the students. The interest of the students in their government was sustained for two elections, or approximately five months.

During the course of the student government, the first election produced a political battle between white candidates and black candidates. The white candidates won. In the second election, with the racial makeup of the group balanced, the students voted for an all black student government. It was interesting to note that although there was a white southerner running for president, the southern students felt that he was incompetent and would not contribute to their welfare if elected, whereas the students on the black ticket were verbal and competent and had a history of performance. The last student government had a white president and a black vice president. The votes showed blacks voting for whites and whites voting for blacks—the destruction of the normal prison racial power which had operated so strongly in the National Training School. Because of a secret ballot and the protection of the individual by the society, there were young men, both black and white, who voted as they pleased rather than by the old pressure system.

About midway through the program, the student government struck against the establishment. The following incident led up to that strike. Because the students were working at a rate which was earning them more than the researchers had anticipated, it was necessary to pull back money from the system by increasing charges for certain services. The weekly room rental rate was raised from six to eight dollars, and a ten dollar weekly food deposit was initiated. At that same time, to create a greater spread in academic performance, the hourly rate was dropped and only academic piece work was paid. These three changes became effective at one time. This was a blunder, but a very useful one.

In our society, the cost of living index goes up bit by bit. If Americans were faced with a 20 per cent increase in the cost of living in one fell swoop, they probably would strike or form a political revolution. But the nature of the system is such that inflation "creeps in this petty pace from day to day" and therefore Americans accept the price rises, although they grumble.

The student body met and decided to strike. They sat down

35

in the lounge and refused to go to work. At this time the director was visiting a project at East St. Louis. He received a call and flew back that very day, asking that the prison officials not enter into the dispute but remain outside the building. It was 9:30 P.M. when the director arrived to meet with the students and their leaders. He was amiable, not angry, and he approached the students in the following manner.

"You guys blew it. You really blew it! I thought you had learned about the powers of government and the powers of protest, but obviously we failed to teach you the use of a strike as a weapon. The unions in America win their demands, but they don't do it by striking first and negotiating later. You have to present your objections and demands first, and ask for negotiations. Then if you don't get the problems resolved, you strike. The strike is the weapon and the last stage in a chain of events. I agree with your viewpoint, but since you've already struck, I have no reason to negotiate with you until after you have returned to work."

The director also pointed out that although the strike was permitted and no one would be punished, in the National Training School this would have been considered a federal offense. He stated that this particular approach of punitive action would not be taken, since CASE acted as a separate community. The students returned to work and a meeting was called. The staff then described why they had to institute the changes. They stated that they had a budget of only one thousand per month, and that expenditure above that figure would jeopardize the length of the project. However, new programs and services were offered so that students could increase their earning power, which was to be utilized in new services rather than commodities. Although earnings were drastically reduced during that week, at no time did anyone remain out of work long enough to place himself in jeopardy—namely, by earning less than the eighteen dollars required to avoid going on relief.

Chapter 3

Design for Learning

$\mathcal{T}$he educational program and the environment which supported it were symbiotic partners in the process of moving the students from defeat to success. The plan for this learning ecology emphasized the relationships between man's behavior and his surroundings. Although consequences influence man's decisions, the physical environment delivers the cues which instruct him. For example, an overhang indicates shelter from a driving rain, and an ashtray on a table indicates that smoking is permitted. Not only do buildings provide protection from the natural elements (rain, snow, insects, and animals), but their planners and builders dictate instructions for their use. The walls, doors, dividers and furniture are behavioral cues for their inhabitants. Although man decides on his space needs, the final form resolution, once established, shapes and continues to maintain a large amount of his behavior.

DESIGN OF THE FACILITY

The following selection from the original grant proposal illustrates the extent of the behavioral approach to the design of the CASE II facility.

A New Learning Environment

Every . . . environment . . . has a physical structure with tools and supply lines that sustain the physical condition. What role does this physical condition play? We know that each physical product says something. A chair says, "sit." A bar across the chair, or a sign saying "ten dollar fine for sitting on this chair," or a "wet paint" sign, does not encourage sitting. The ability of the individual to sit on the chair (the demonstration of a sitting behavior) is directly dependent upon two aspects of the condition: (1) the physical object, chair, and (2) the contingencies that maintain or restrict the behavior (the bar, the fine, the destruction of the clothing by wet paint). The contingencies govern the behavior of the one who wishes to sit on the physical object chair. It is not just the tool itself (the physical product)—whether it be a building, a group of buildings, a chair, a laboratory table, a film, a book—that maintains a complex behavior of learning, but the nature and the extent of the consequences. There are cases wherein the architectural condition does define and limit the use of its facility. A glass or marble wall clearly states, "You cannot put a thumb tack in me." On the other hand, a paperboard or celotex wall says, "Yes, you can." However, the physical conditions—the walls, ceilings, floors, chairs, and tables—in combination with the moving chain in the environment—the teachers, students, books, and supplies—are a complex interaction maintained for the most part by the frequency and the extent of the reinforcers: the rewards, the immediate or long range goals [Cohen, 1964].

Seven project functions were used as points of departure for the development of the actual procedures employed during the CASE II project: the student office, the lecture hall/laboratory, the private sleeping room, the cafeteria, the lounge, the library, and the store.

In order to study, a student requires light, privacy from visual and physical interruption, books, paper, a surface to write upon, and a place to sit. The SER office fulfilled the following objectives: The office with the student's name on the wall provided a sense of personal privacy and pride, as well as an area of staff control. It provided an isolated environment wherein beginning study behaviors were programed. It also provided a place for special teaching machine scheduling. The student could use it as a center for communication between himself and his teachers and he could store some of his textual and three-dimensional school materials there. It was a place where visual controls were added and removed, where disciplines relevant to reading, writing, and coordination of information were controlled. The space was used as a reinforcer—a rental piece of property worth a required amount (90 per cent or better performance) of basic academic behaviors. Less than this prescribed performance meant the loss of a student's right to have an office. It was a basic tool in helping the student to learn self-discipline.

Educational activities are generally filled with behaviors requiring different stimuli (books, films, materials, space, teacher, other students) in particular temporal and spatial arrangements. Some activities require two people (oral reading, a speaker and a listener); some require more than two (a group needed to fulfill a complex physics lab experiment). There are also some activities in which an increase in quantity of human beings does not basically detract from a learning activity (a lecture, a lecture demonstration, a film) and therefore can be scheduled successfully in groups. The lecture hall/laboratory was often combined in this demonstration project to take advantage of all known uses of group learning and group reinforcement. The environment was programed for film, tapes, slides, and live lectures and was subsequently scheduled so as to act differentially for the variety of subject matter to be taught in the curriculum.

The way in which the student organized and maintained his private living-sleeping quarters and the visual images he selected to decorate it were used to measure a variety of things; in particular, cultural change. The schedule for work or leisure in his own space—its use and the friends he permitted to visit in his space—became another means of measuring social change. Regulations governing visiting other rooms were maintained and a time schedule for floor use permitted ample control.

A New Learning Environment

The availability of a variety of foods in the cafeteria allowed the student to choose again. By raising or lowering prices, quantities, and methods of display, the staff introduced many new foods to students. Names of foods and language usage were further reinforced by wall signs and daily menus. Special Sunday and Saturday evening dinners with family or special visitors were used to teach table manners and socially useful behaviors normal to a semiformal eating situation; for example, proper clothing, general grooming, conversation, and table etiquette.

The word *lounge* connotes enjoyment—a nonacademic reinforcement, the place where one goes to dance, listen to teenage music, talk about "regular stuff," and get away from school. The lounge remained a teen town setup, but slowly other kinds of music, activities, and visuals were introduced into the environment. Through successive approximation, the lounge was reshaped to act as a reinforcer for the academic and vocational behaviors as well as the acceptable social behaviors.

The establishment of the library adjacent to the actual lounge permitted the staff to shape up alternatives to playing the jukebox, cards, and so on. By using the fading procedures used in CASE I, CASE II increased the students' use of the library for reading newspapers, magazines, and books; here they could also play games that helped reinforce decision and problem-solving behaviors which were introduced in the programed educational work week.

The store, through carefully selected purchasing and by recording types, quantity, and time of purchase, became the arbiter of taste and the cultural change agency. By creating "sales" and a means of displaying items for immediate availability, the store was able to provide the stimulus for a way of life.

The Federal Bureau of Prisons provided the project with elemental services and facilities. The major contribution was Jefferson Hall, an unused, four-story, fireproof structure which had previously housed approximately one hundred inmates. It was one of the newest buildings on the grounds (though several decades old) and was found to be quite suitable for the project environmental requirements. Considerable planning was required, however, to redesign the existing space into a unit which would accommodate all functions of the project.

Each of the four floors housed a semi-autonomous program function. This general plan allowed for the most advantageous utilization of existing facilities and provided for the student control necessary in this penal situation. The ground floor of Jefferson Hall (Figure 1) contained the thirty specially constructed sleeping rooms (Area A), each six by eight feet. Area B was used for the minimum rental (relief status) sleeping and storage facility. Bunks and wall lockers were provided for those students who did not wish to rent private rooms. Area C was used for a nighttime cottage officer control station. Area D was furnished as a lavatory and provided with lockable storage units for personal hygiene articles. Area E was the communal shower. Each shower was provided with an individual faucet control. Private lockable shower stalls and a bathtub were installed as shown on the outside wall. Area F was used for a linen and bed clothing storage and distribution center. Area G was the stairwell and hallway leading to the first floor. It could be isolated from the sleeping quarters by the lockable door which separated the two areas.

The first floor of Jefferson Hall (Figure 2) contained the dining facility, the purchasing and recreation area, and research staff offices. Area A was the planning staff office. It provided private space for the associate project director and the nighttime research assistant. Area B was the principal investigator's office and conference room. The C areas were for supportive staff and also data control work stations. This included work areas for one secretary/receptionist, one typist/bookkeeper, and two data control analysts. Area D was a waiting room for visitors. Area E was employed alternately as a dining hall, movie hall, coffee break room, and television room. The counter top shown in this area was provided by the food service contractor and housed steam tables and other relevant food dispensing equipment. Area F was the kitchen. It was provided with a pantry, utensil storage, stainless steel counter tops, and a wash sink; an institutional size refrigerator, range, and dish-

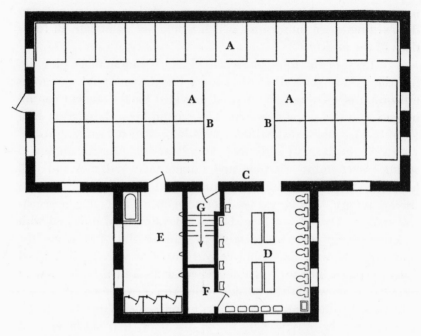

FIGURE 1.   Ground Floor (Basement), 3400 square feet

washer were also included. The entire room was under the direct control of the food service manager, supervised by the CASE II dietetic consultant and the CASE II staff. This kitchen had a separate outside entrance to ensure hygienic food handling and a non-disruptive means of entrance to and exit from this floor.

Area G, the store, served as the major control center for the student-oriented operations of this floor. Area H was the lounge, or recreation center. The doorway between the lounge and the ante-chamber facing the store was outfitted with a turnstile to facilitate control over lounge entrance. The library in Area I provided space for reading and quiet leisure games and activities, such as chess and Scrabble. (Later this area became a TV room and the library was moved to the education floor.) The front door of the library remained closed except for emergencies. The side door was the only entrance. Area J was the lavatory facility for this floor. Area K enclosed the first floor hall and stairwell leading to the ground floor and third floor. This area was controlled by the lockable doors on the ground floor, at the outside rear entry, and at the head of the stairs shown on the second floor plan.

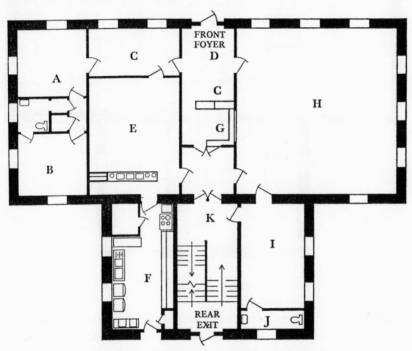

FIGURE 2. First Floor, 3400 square feet

The second floor of Jefferson Hall (Figure 3) was utilized for most of the educational activities that were provided within the CASE II project. Area A was used for an auditorium and lecture hall. It was outfitted with standard student desks. The flexible divider partitioned this six hundred square foot auditorium into two smaller classrooms. (The smaller section became the library area part way through the program.) Area B was the audiovisual recording and presentation center. It provided the means by which audio and visual information from either one or both of the two rooms was gathered and presented. Area C contained three automatic testing

43

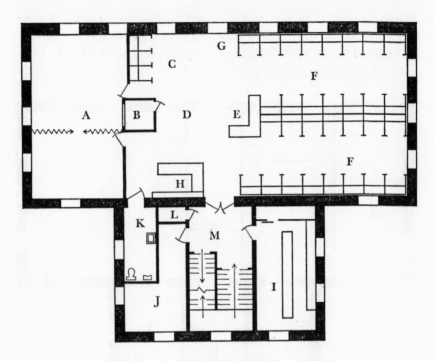

FIGURE 3.   Second Floor, 3400 square feet

booth systems. These were employed only for those educational progress examinations for which automatic programing had been established. The equipment used for the programing of these booths was located in Area I. Area D was furnished with open tables and was employed as a nonautomated testing room. Area E was a reference book area provided with all pertinent materials. The students did prime research with these books at this station only. Area F housed thirty private study offices, each four feet square. Each private office contained a desk surface, a lockable storage file, a wastebasket, a study chair, and a clip-on-lamp. The student used this office for all programed study units, textual reading, composition writing, and so on. Area G was designed as an entrance from the education floor onto the roof of the front porch of Jefferson Hall, which was used for conducting biological experiments in season and for housing special

44

projects, such as aviary. Area H was used as the control center for the educational floor. The time-clock for this floor was located at this station. Area I contained the educational program-checking stations and housed the programing equipment for the testing booths. During the hours assigned for personal study, subject matter specialists manned stations in this room to check programs, assign testing materials, check hand-scored tests, assign new programs, and counsel on the status of the student's educational progress. Area J was used as a wet shop for science experiments and other projects which required the utilization of a laboratory area. Area K was employed as the lavatory facility for the second floor. Area L was controlled by the staff member located at Area H. Materials such as typewriters and teaching machines were distributed from this storage area. Area M included the second floor landing and stairwells leading down to the first floor and up to the third floor. Access to these stairs was controlled by the double lockable door leading down and the single lockable door leading up.

The third floor of Jefferson Hall (Figure 4) was utilized for vocational workshops, laboratories, counseling and psychiatric space, and teachers' offices. Area A was a heavy trade vocational workshop (for developing such skills as carpentry, cabinetmaking, and plumbing). It was provided with all necessary work surfaces, storage, and equipment. Area B was a technical vocational workshop (for developing such skills as electronics and drafting). It was provided with all necessary equipment, including a photographic print dryer to service the darkroom. Area C was a small class seminar room provided with all necessary educational furnishings. Area D was a film preview room and teachers' conference area. Area E served as an office for four part-time teachers. Area F was equipped as a photographic darkroom for project use and for a vocational workshop in this trade area. Area G was used primarily for storage. It served as the observer's station (through one-way glass) for the adjacent counseling room and housed all pertinent tape recording and electronic equipment. Area H was the psychiatric/counseling room for the project and was furnished accordingly. Area I was the women's lavatory.

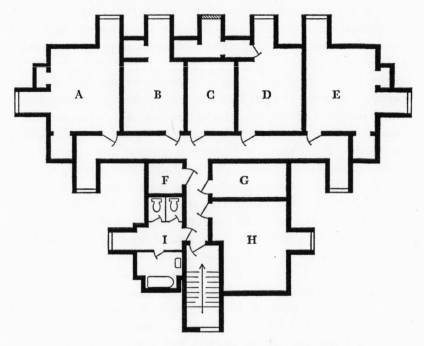

FIGURE 4.   Third Floor, approximately 2440 square feet

This environmental plan was developed to allow for a maximum explication of the program functions described earlier. Although this plan was quite completely prepared it was not inflexible and modifications could be made while the project was in progress.

EDUCATIONAL PROGRAM

After orientation and testing, the student was placed at a starting point in all curriculum areas. He was also given the examination on the CASE II procedures based on the Handbook. After achieving 90 per cent or better on this examination the student was given a private study office and entered the educational process (of the forty-one students, only one did not pass this examination on his first try). Programed learning, which formed the heart of this process, was maintained by the CASE II project in two ways: through auto-instruction and in programed courses.

An auto-instruction (self-instruction) program is a self-contained set of material on a specific subject (such as English grammar, introductory algebra, or physics). The program includes a set of frames, each of which is presented as a separate item of information. The student reads the frame and responds by answering a question or filling in a blank. For example, the following frame with a word missing would be read:

Here is a complete sentence of only two words: Children eat. *We know that this sentence is about* ——— *who do something.*

The student completes a statement or answers a question based on information in the preceding step. After he records his answer (by writing on a separate sheet of paper or by pressing a button on a mechanical device), a system of reinforcement is used. The answer is exposed and he learns that *children* is the answer.

A succeeding frame would present the answer and a reworded sentence reexplaining the principle. Again, a word would be omitted.

Children. . . .
Children eat *is a sentence, but the word* children *by itself is not a* ———.

The student is learning in a step-by-step sequence which builds upon his preliminary vocabulary and information and introduces new information with a check on his understanding of that information before he can proceed. The next frame would introduce the learning item in another way:

The word children *by itself merely names a topic that we might talk about. To make a sentence of it, we must tell something about what* ——— *do.*

Each lesson (set of material) proceeds one step at a time (frame by frame) and permits the student to reason his way through the material, rather than being told what to think. Thus, the explanations of information are interwoven with exercising knowledge of that information. Both thinking and attention are actively involved, and the student is reinforced (rewarded) in very small steps.

This system of independent working through a set of material is based upon the Socratic method of question and answer or problem and solution and has been expanded through Edward Thorndike's Law of Effect, experimental analysis, and B. F. Skinner's operant conditioning. S. L. Pressey, a major contributor to this method, instrumented a device for multiple-choice testing which could be self-scored. His principle of immediate feedback facilitating progression at the student's own pace was further expanded upon by R. C. Peterson, who prepared chemically treated answer sheets and a special marking pencil. Leslie J. Briggs devised a twenty-answer multiple-choice subject-matter-trainer for the Air Force. Skinner, emphasizing recall instead of multiple-choice, devised one of the best known devices for employing visibility of one question at a time. An adjacent correct answer was made visible after the student had completed his answer and then exposed the succeeding frame with the correct answer. Many other persons have continued to devise instrumentation based upon the principal work of Pressey and Skinner (see Lumsdaine and Glaser, 1960).

The self-contained auto-instruction program can be a labor-saving device for the student as well as the instructor. The student is not held to a lock step method of learning and thus bored by the slow pace of some students and the speed of others. His achievements depend on understanding rather than on timing. He is actively engaged in learning, frame by frame, and does not proceed until he understands the material. Through the development of the sequenced program, with its hinting, prompting, and cuing, the student is directed toward the correct answers and is reinforced through immediate feedback. Thus, he is more likely to remain alert and busy through sustained activity.

The instructor directs learning and confers with individuals on specific aspects of the program. Instead of teaching an entire lesson which some of the students may already know, the instructor can supply supplementary information, answer individual questions, grade unit tests, or discuss other facets of the lesson. The instructor's role as drillmaster is changed. Aversive control is eliminated.

In *The Technology of Teaching,* Skinner (1968) qualifies the contribution of the teaching machine:

The machine . . . simply brings the student into contact with the person who composed the material it presents. It is a labor-saving device because it can bring one programer into contact with an indefinite number of students. This may suggest mass production, but the effect upon each student is surprisingly like that of a private tutor. The comparison holds in several respects. (1) There is a constant interchange between program and student. Unlike lectures, textbooks, and the usual audiovisual aids, the machine induces sustained activity. The student is always alert and busy. (2) Like a good tutor, the machine insists that a given point be thoroughly understood, either frame by frame or set by set, before the student moves on. Lectures, textbooks, and their mechanized equivalents, on the other hand, proceed without making sure that the student understands and easily leave him behind. (3) Like a good tutor the machine presents just that material for which the student is ready. It asks him to take only that step which he is at the moment best equipped and most likely to take. (4) Like a skillful tutor the machine helps the student to come up with the right answer. It does this in part through the orderly construction of the program and in part with such techniques as hinting, prompting, and suggesting, derived from an analysis of verbal behavior. (5) Lastly, of course, the machine, like the private tutor, reinforces the student for every correct response, using this immediate feedback not only to shape his behavior most efficiently but to maintain it in strength in a manner which the layman would describe as "holding the student's interest."

A programed course is a prepared set of material on a specific subject which incorporates the sequential approach to subject matter in a classroom. Pre- and post-tests, group discussion and lecture, individual study in workbook and reading assignments, and audiovisual aids (films, slides, tapes, and so on) are related to the terminal objectives.

The programed materials used for CASE II provided a wide variety of subject matter which ranged from the second through the twelfth levels of conventional academic grades. Starting with approximately twenty-five programs used for CASE I and CASE I Interim work with the students, the CASE II project expanded this number to 126 during its term. The five subject matter areas— reading, language usage, mathematics, science and technology, and social studies—were divided into four academic groupings: freshman (grades 1, 2, 3, 4); sophomore (grades 5, 6, 7); junior (grades 8, 9, 10A); and senior (grades 10B, 11, 12).

The CASE I project chose programs on the basis of the publisher's statement concerning grade level suitability—from fourth through sixth grade. Even though materials were purchased which covered levels below and above this range, a very large area remained to be filled for the CASE II curriculum. It was also found, in working with the programed materials during the CASE I project, that the publisher's grade level recommendations did not necessarily apply to the CASE population. Many programs were reviewed, and it was found that the use of criterion frames (or test frames) within the program units was essential. Each unit needed a test which the student had to pass before going on to the next unit. Well-programed materials which had these features were preferred over those that did not. Programs that were written sequentially with other programs were also generally found to be more useful than those listed by the publisher as separate programs.

Many of the commercially available programs purchased did not have criterion frames, separate units, or tests for the individual units. This meant that once a program arrived from the publisher, hours of preparation were required before it could be used. When a program needed modification, a teacher reviewed it thoroughly, deleted certain frame answers, and recorded the changes. If the program needed unit breakdown, this was done and a test was prepared for each unit. After point values had been determined, the program was approved for trial use by a few students. The student behaviors were monitored while the students were working on the new modified program. If additional changes were indicated, the program was removed from service until those changes were made.

Program tests presented another problem. Most publishers provide only one version of each program test. When a student failed to reach 90 per cent on a first testing, he reviewed and then took a second test. With only one test provided for each program, there was no assurance that the student had not simply remembered the correct responses from the initial testing and review. To eliminate this problem, the staff made alternate forms of each examination by scrambling and rewording the questions.

All programed materials were assigned a point value before being placed in use. Some general guidelines for assessing a program's point value were established on the basis of experience in the CASE I project. Once a program had been reviewed and the necessary changes made, a breakdown was made of unit frames and the number of questions for each examination.

For example, a value of four points was tentatively assigned for each 10 unit frames: a unit consisting of 210 frames would be assigned a value of eighty-four points. The values of all the units were then totaled, and this amount was used to determine the value placed on the program tests. The point value of a program was divided so that less than 50 per cent would be issued for successful completion of the unit materials and more than 50 per cent for successful test taking. Approximately one-fourth of all the points available for successful testing were assigned to the program post-test. The biggest payoff was for testing and for program post-testing in particular. It should also be noted that the assigned point values for both the program units and tests were the maximum value. A student scoring 96 per cent accuracy would receive only 96 per cent of this maximum assigned value. After a program had been assigned point values, it was evaluated on the basis of student performance time and difficulty in obtaining 90 per cent accuracy. The student earned points in both the self-instructional programs and the programed courses.

Programed courses were used as prerequisites for certain classes or seminars, and, additionally, the completion of certain programs was required for promotion to the next academic level. For example, two spelling programs, a program in dictionary usage, and a grammar program were required in the freshman language usage area before a student could be considered for promotion to the sophomore level. The other freshman curriculum areas also had programs which required completion before a student could be promoted to the next level. For certain classes, such as the Jet-Set Science class taught in November and December, the students were required to have at least a sophomore standing in the curriculum area of science and technology skills. This meant that they were required to have completed at least three science courses. It was also recommended that they be working on a junior level program in this same area.

A total of sixteen classes were taught during CASE II (see Table 1). All classes required a small registration or laboratory fee. Three of these classes were in the reading curriculum; two of these were specifically developed for remedial reading. Three classes were in the language and communication skills area; one of these was a night class in typing which required a 2500 point registration fee. Two classes were in mathematics and four were in science and technology. Four courses were in social systems skills. With two exceptions—freshman classes in reading and mathematics—all classes were at the sophomore-junior level.

Preparation for the first CASE II class, American history, began during January 1966. Two teachers and the chaplain were assigned by the CASE director to develop the course. These three NTS staff members had participated in the staff training sessions conducted during the CASE I project. They were familiarized with the basic methods of instructional programing, and they were assisted by the project's research staff.

An ongoing critique of the American history class was conducted by the teachers and a full evaluation was made upon com-

Design for Learning

Table 1. CASE II SCHEDULE OF CLASSROOM COURSES

Day Classes	Dates
1. How to Form a Student Government	Jan. 24–Jan. 28, 1966
2. The American Revolution	Jan. 25–Mar. 11, 1966
3. Visual Language	Feb. 22–Mar. 11, 1966
4. Telephone Class	May 16–May 27, 1966
5. Basic Teachings of Religion	June 14–Aug. 30, 1966
6. Reading Clinic	Oct. 10, 1966–Feb. 2, 1967
7. Arithmetic Clinic	Oct. 11, 1966–Feb. 2, 1967
8. English and American Literature	Nov. 9, 1966–Jan. 27, 1967
9. Jet-Set Science	Nov. 15, 1966–Jan. 26, 1967
10. Physiology Laboratory	Nov. 22, 1966–Feb. 2, 1967
11. Earth Geography	Nov. 28, 1966–Feb. 3, 1967
12. Listen and Read	Dec. 14, 1966–Feb. 1, 1967
13. Advanced Math Clinic	Jan. 5–Jan. 26, 1967

Evening Classes	
14. Typing	Mar. 16–May 18, 1966
15. Electricity and Electronics	May 26–July 5, 1966
16. Design	Dec. 8–Dec. 29, 1966

pletion of the class. Both the advantages and disadvantages were noted. It was decided that the class could have been shortened and integrated with several commercially available programed units.

The procedures used for development of the history class proved valuable to the NTS staff. Subsequently, the chaplain designed a class in the basic teachings of religion for the CASE project and he used programed instruction and other techniques he had learned during the preparation of the history class. This same class in religion was then taught by the chaplain to the entire NTS population as a regular part of his Sunday school sessions.

Numerous short-term courses, or seminars, were also held during the first half of the project. One of these was for an advanced student who completed a literature course, Franklin Through Frost, presented over a local educational television station. He was paid points for successful completion of tests but did not pay an entrance fee.

The programs, courses, and classes formed the basic learning structure in CASE II. The process of utilizing this structure is illustrated by the routine a typical entering student went through during the later months of the project. The educational coordinator discussed all of the student's pre-test scores with him and showed him his relative placement on the total curriculum chart. The student was classified as a freshman, sophomore, junior or senior on the basis of his overall test results. He was given a choice of several programs in each of the different subject areas and was told that a very careful check would be made of his initial progress to insure that he had been properly placed. If the programs selected for his starting point were either too difficult or below his level of accomplishment, his placement was changed or he was given supplementary programs. He was shown how to work through the two basic types of auto-instructional programs (linear and intrinsic) in a step-by-step fashion. He was also told that he was free to work concurrently on several programs but that certain programs were required before he could be promoted to the next academic level. Furthermore, completion of the individual unit currently assigned was required before he could work on a different program.

The student could take breaks from his work whenever he desired, but he was required to "clock out" of the program when doing so. The importance of this accuracy in recording work time was stressed. The student was shown the CASE II educational program flow chart (see Figure 5)—which was posted in the testing room and in the program checking area—and the procedures he was required to follow were explained.

After a student had completed a unit of work he took it, along with his written answers, to a program checker at the program checking station. The program checker reviewed all test-frame answers or, if the program had no test frames, he questioned the student concerning the materials covered. If a student achieved 85 to 89 per cent on either his written test-frame answers or on the oral

Design for Learning

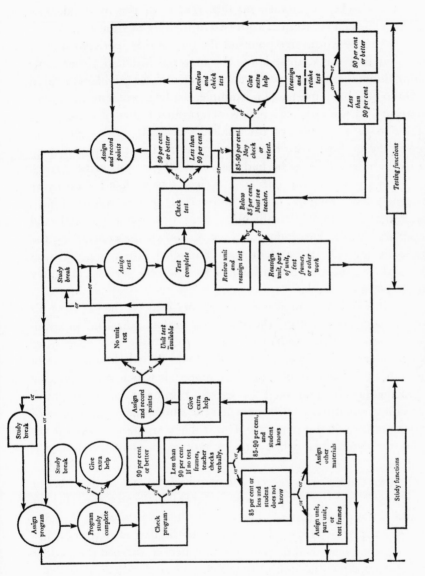

FIGURE 5.   CASE II Educational Program Flow Chart

quiz, the checker conducted an oral review of the material. The student was then confronted with two branching possibilities.

A score within five points of the required 90 per cent usually indicated that the student knew the material but had either some minor difficulties with a particular aspect of it or problems related to different subject matter (for example, reading problems in a math program). If the checker's review determined either of these possibilities to be the cause of the student's difficulty, the student reviewed the problem with the staff member and was permitted to go on to the next step as if he had passed at 90 per cent or better.

If, however, the checker's review session (and these were extremely brief reviews, usually under four or five minutes) indicated that the student's difficulties were not minor but reflected some basic misunderstanding or lack of knowledge concerning the materials studied, the student was channeled into the procedures followed by students who had scored less than 85 per cent accuracy on the program check.

If a student scored less than 85 per cent on the check of his test-frame answers or on the checker's verbal quiz, the program checker returned the student to the first step in the flow chart after assigning him one of two alternatives: redo the whole unit, part of the unit, or the test frames; or study materials which would provide supplemental or additional background information. The latter procedure was usually followed when the student had a basic lack of understanding of the material. The teacher or the educational coordinator determined what type of supplemental materials would be used.

A student who scored the required 90 per cent or better on his test frames or quiz was congratulated, and the checker recorded the points earned. The student then continued in the educational sequence in one of two ways. If the unit of materials successfully completed had no post-test, the checker assigned the student to the next sequential unit of material. The student took these back to his study area and began the study process again. If the material had a unit test, the student was assigned to the testing room. When the student reported to the testing room, the tester recorded his entry time and unit test assignment and gave him the appropriate test form. The student then took his examination in one of the testing stations and returned to the tester with his paper. The tester immediately checked the student's answers.

A score of at least 90 per cent was again required for the student to continue on in the program sequence. If a student did not do this well, but did achieve a score of at least 85 per cent, the tester held a brief review session and assigned him an alternate form of the same test. When the student finished, the tester immediately checked it. If the student scored at least 90 per cent on this retest, he passed to the next step in the program sequence. If the student scored below 90 per cent on this retake, he was handled as if he had scored below 85 per cent on the original test.

A student who scored below 85 per cent on a unit test was assigned to a teacher or to the educational coordinator. The outcome of this interview varied and depended on the teacher's assessment of the student's difficulty. Minimally, the teacher reviewed the unit material or the specific test material and assigned the student to be retested. If the teacher determined that the student needed more work than could be provided by a review, the student was reassigned to the unit, part of the unit, the test frames of the unit, or some supplemental program work. In these instances the student was recycled to the first position in the flow chart and began the process again, working his way toward the testing session. No points were issued for any test on which the student scored below the 90 per cent accuracy level. A student who scored the required 90 per cent or better on his test was congratulated by the tester and had his point earnings recorded. After that achievement, he returned to the program checking station to obtain the next study materials in his program sequence. The program completion process then began again.

The student could take a break from this process at any point. However, if he left the testing room before completing his assigned test, the test was scored at whatever level of completion the student left it. To check out for a break a student simply turned in his study materials at the program checking station. The checker then clocked him out of work. When the student wished to restart, he reported back to the checker and was clocked into work and given his materials. Students were required to turn in all of their assigned study materials when they left for lunch and at the close of the day.

A student who was having difficulty with his educational programs could request an interview with any member of the staff. Generally, all such interviews were first scheduled with the educational coordinator. If the student did not feel that he had received a satisfactory resolution of the problem, he could request an interview with the assistant director, associate director, or project director. Most problems were settled shortly after the interview, but others were considered in longer range planning. Interviews were also arranged with the caseworker and consulting psychiatric personnel. These were relatively infrequent and usually led to mild disruptions when the student returned to the educational area. For example, if a student was notified of an approved parole date, he usually stopped on his way back from the interview to mention this to all of his friends while they were studying in their offices, and their vocal approval was quite apparent.

The codification of procedures for use of instructional materials was invaluable. The specific procedures were outlined and displayed for both student and educational staff, making it possible to routinize most educational decisions. There was little possibility for procedural misguidance by a member of the staff when he was performing program assignment, checking, or testing duties. The majority of interpretive decisions were made by a member of the teaching staff qualified to review and recommend alternate methods regarding specific subject matter topics. Because these procedures were eminently available for scrutiny, staff decisions regarding a student's progress through study programs could not be construed by the student as prejudicial or unwarranted. One set of procedures applied consistently for all students in all study programs.

The procedures were tightly specified and consistent, but there was considerable variation and freedom in the kinds of behavior available to the students. Each student was free to work or not to work and free to work at anything in which he had demonstrated the necessary level of preparation. Pay was contingent only on performance, a constraint which differed from the requirements of the "outside" only in the consistency of the specification that the performance be competent. Mechanisms were available to the students for improving the system, for using it more or less efficiently, and for protest.

Chapter 4

General Operation

$\mathcal{T}$he total CASE project schedule antedated and postdated the time when students participated. The CASE Interim Period began at the termination of formal CASE I activities on October 31, 1965, and continued until the CASE II facility opened formally on February 4, 1966. The Interim Period was used for planning and preparation of programs, procedures, and facilities for CASE II. Half-day educational operations also were conducted for students. A special data schedule for CASE II was in effect from the date of opening until February 3, 1967, and with minor specific exceptions the project systems and data described here cover this one-year period. A variety of records was kept on each CASE II student during his stay. These records exist for all project functions during this year in which twenty-four-hour control was maintained.

The period of time from the end of this special data schedule until May 30 was designated the CASE II Project Closing Period. Post-project testing was in process from February 3 until February 10. All CASE students began attending the ERA educational program at the NTS (which we designed and supervised) on February

General Operation

13, 1967, but they continued to live at Jefferson Hall, within the environment of CASE II. They participated in the NTS educational program from 7:00 A.M. to 3:45 P.M., Monday through Friday. The other aspects of the project continued operating until March 22, 1967, when the students were transferred to the NTS population.

Because CASE II was an outgrowth of the CASE I project, the students previously assigned to CASE I were included in the CASE II population. And, like CASE I students, the CASE II students were not volunteers to the project. Therefore, they were not necessarily well motivated for academic study. The additional students assigned were chosen so as to develop a more accurate sampling of the total inmate population profile of the NTS.

The mean student population for the project was slightly more than twenty-five students, with a 50.5 per cent Negro and 49.5 per cent white population. On January 1, 1966, the NTS reported a population of 46.9 per cent Negro and 50.6 per cent white. One year later the NTS indicated a population of 52.5 per cent Negro, 45.0 per cent white, and 2.5 per cent of American Indian or other racial background. The CASE II racial population fell within this reported range of racial distribution.

Although the proposal stated a concern with a northern and southern regional division, the project intake was primarily divided on the basis of whether a student was a Federal commitment or from the District of Columbia. (Federal students came from various parts of the country and had committed federal offenses. The others were sent to prison from the District of Columbia; were, with one exception, black; and most had committed crimes against person.) The Federal/District population of the NTS was estimated at approximately 50 per cent each. Hence, this was the percentage that was attempted by the project. Actual figures for the NTS for the year 1966–1967 indicate a range of 57.2 per cent to 55.4 per cent for Federal commitments and a range of 40.7 per cent to 41.2 per cent for District of Columbia commitments. The CASE II student popu-

61

lation based on the mean of the end-of-the-month figures indicates 52.51 per cent Federal and 47.49 per cent District of Columbia commitments.

It was not possible to predict when students would enter the NTS or what types of students would be assigned to NTS. Therefore, it was agreed that when a vacancy occurred at CASE II the next student assigned to the NTS who fit the racial or Federal/District category criteria would be assigned to the project. A further listing of the project's population is provided in Table 2. The NTS figures concerning offense type for January 1, 1967, are similar to those of CASE II. The NTS indicates 52.5 per cent commitments for "auto theft," 23.4 per cent for "other against property," and 24.1 per cent "other against person."

Table 2. OFFENSES COMMITTED BY CASE II STUDENTS

Type of Offense	CASE II Population	
	Number	Per Cent
Dyer Act (auto theft)	18	43.9
Housebreaking	4	9.8
Postal violations	2	4.9
Petty larceny	3	7.3
Robbery	3	7.3
Assault	3	7.3
Homicide	1	2.4
Other	7	17.1
Totals	41	100.0

Table 3 provides characteristics upon entry that are descriptive of the forty-one students who participated in CASE II as a group.

STUDENT ORIENTATION

All seventeen students who entered the CASE II project on February 4, 1966, had been actively engaged, on a half-day basis

Table 3. CHARACTERISTICS AT ENTRY

Variable	Mean	Standard Deviation
Age at entry into CASE II (years)	16.9	0.88
Length of sentence (years)	2.7	1.38
Previous grade completed	7.9	1.15
Median SAT grade score at entry	5.7	2.16
Mean SAT grade score at entry	5.73	2.11
Entry IQ score (Revised Beta)	93.47	9.98
Gates Reading Survey grade score at entry	6.39	2.57

during the month of January, in the readying of Jefferson Hall. Although they were becoming acquainted during that month with what the program would offer and require, on Saturday, February 5, a two-hour orientation class explaining the project in detail was held. They were issued Handbooks and at the close of the class were given the orientation examination. Each incoming CASE II student was required to go through a functionally similar orientation program which was designed to familiarize him with CASE procedures.

When a vacancy occurred in the CASE population, the NTS Office of Classification and Parole reviewed its newly assigned students and selected those who would be sent to CASE. When a student arrived at the NTS, he was sent to the hospital for physical and dental checkups. After those examinations were completed, the student was brought to Jefferson Hall.

The new student had little or no contact with the general NTS population. During his first morning at Jefferson Hall, he was given a tour of the facility and taken into the CASE lounge; the CASE associate or assistant director briefed him on the history, goals, and procedures of the project and gave him the SER Handbook. Following the initial interview each student had a personal interview with the project director. This interview served three purposes: a short personal history of the student was gathered, the

63

student was introduced to "the man," and the student was made aware of the project operation. The interviews with the project director and associate director usually took up the entire two hour and fifteen minute period available before lunch. Shortly before the noon meal each new student was introduced to the officers of the student government, who took him to lunch and introduced him to other students.

During the afternoon study period, the new student began his orientation testing battery, including Stanford Achievement Test, Gates Reading Survey, and approximately forty other post-tests from auto-instructional programs used in the educational area. The completion of this entire testing series took between five and seven days. During this lengthy testing battery, the student was given breaks for learning how to use the auto-instructional programs and machines, for short lectures on CASE operations, reading his Handbook, and interviews with the educational coordinator and staff. Within the first four days, the staff was able to make a relatively accurate assessment of the student's academic ability and interest to guide him into a core of beginning programed material.

Following his first evening meal the new student had an instructional session with the chief of data control and banking. During this session, a detailed explanation was given of the CASE point system, means of earning points, payroll procedures, and procedures for ordering room and meal plans for the week. Subsequently, the student could apply for an entrance loan which paid for his first full week's room and board and allotted him a basic number of points to spend. When the student had completed his interview with data control and banking, he received his private room assignment on the home floor and a stock of free toilet articles and cigarettes to use during his first few days in the project. Each new student was given several days of free room and board, depending on when he entered the project. That is, the number of days between his entrance and the first payday were free.

When the student moved into his private room that evening, the correctional officer on duty had an informal interview with him. The officer stressed the need to understand project operations in detail and counseled the student to read the SER Handbook which outlined all material the student needed to know to operate well within the project. The student was informed that within two weeks he would be permitted to take a test on the Handbook, and that when he achieved 90 per cent or better on that test he would be allowed to participate in outdoor sports and would be assigned a private study office on the educational floor.

Following the student's completion of the orientation testing and assignment to educational programs, he was scheduled for a series of interviews with CASE and NTS staff members. These interviews were with the chaplain and psychologist from NTS and the correctional supervisor, educational coordinator, and caseworker from CASE. The interview reports and observations of student behavior were used to develop summaries of the student's prognosis within the project. All of the summaries were subsequently reviewed by the CASE Committee for Student Affairs. Then the caseworker was required to prepare the student classifications study, using these summaries and other information supplied by the courts. This classification study was reviewed by the Youth Division parole authorities and the student was scheduled for a hearing before them within the first two months of his stay. The results of the Youth Division review and hearing were referred back to the student on an administrative "yellow sheet" within sixty days of the date of the hearing. They could recommend either continuance in the proposed program until the next specified hearing date or parole at a specified time.

A TYPICAL PROJECT DAY

During data Period IV, a typical project day began between 6:00 A.M. and 8:00 A.M. The students were responsible for waking and preparing themselves for a day of school. Breakfast began at 7:30 A.M., when freshmen were served. Sophomores were served at 7:40 A.M., juniors at 7:50 A.M., and seniors at 7:55 A.M. The cafeteria closed at 8:15 A.M. At its closing all remaining students went into the lounge, which had also opened at 7:30 A.M. During the period from 7:30 A.M. until 8:30 A.M., the students had free admission to the lounge and free television. At 8:00 A.M. those students who wanted to go on sick call were taken to the NTS Hospital.

When the educational area opened at 8:30 A.M., the students went directly from the lounge to spend the remainder of the morning on the various study programs. They worked on programed instruction, took tests, went to classes, spent time in tutorial sessions with teachers, or went into the library/free area. At 11:45 A.M. the students moved downstairs to the home floor. They had fifteen minutes to relax, tidy rooms, or clean up before lunch was served at 12:00 noon. Procedures at lunchtime were similar to those at breakfast, except that the order in which the students ate was reversed. The students entered the cafeteria at five-minute intervals, with the seniors starting at 12:00 noon. The cafeteria closed at 12:45 P.M. and, as they had done after breakfast, all students went to the lounge. The lounge opened at the start of the lunch period, with free admission. From 1:00 P.M. until 1:30 P.M., the students could choose to remain in the lounge, to return to the home floor, or—when weather permitted and staff was available—to go outdoors for recreation.

School began again at 1:30 P.M., and the students continued the routine of the morning academic session. They also could leave the educational area at 3:00 P.M. and go into the lounge. However, from 3:00 P.M. to 5:00 P.M. the lounge charged a rather costly hourly fee of one hundred points. The lounge remained open until 5:00 P.M., when any students remaining there went either to the cafeteria for dinner or to the home floor. Although the educational area remained open until 4:30 P.M., several days each week the students had the option of leaving the educational floor at 4:00 P.M. for approximately one hour of outdoor recreation. All remaining students left the educational floor at 4:30 P.M. and went downstairs to the home floor. During this half-hour before dinner, the students attended to a variety of personal activities. Shortly before 5:00 P.M. the students who had been outside returned to the home floor. The seniors ate at 5:00, juniors at 5:10, sophomores at 5:15, and freshmen at 5:20 P.M.

General Operation

From the time the cafeteria closed at 6:00 P.M. until lights out at 10:00 P.M., the students chose their own activities. The store opened for sales at 6:00 P.M., and at 6:30 P.M. the storekeeper supervised operations of the lounge which reopened. The library opened at 6:00 P.M. and provided book browsing and check-out, scheduled educational television programs, supervised hobby and craft activities and—starting at 7:00 P.M.—supervision and assistance with some study activities in regular program work. Unless a scheduled television program was in progress, the library closed at 9:00 P.M. On certain nights of the week the students were able to participate in activities at the NTS gym from 6:30 P.M. until 8:00 P.M. Several students also held part-time jobs within the project and worked from 7:00 to 9:00 P.M.

From 4:30 P.M., when the educational area was closed, the home floor remained open and all students were to be there by 10:00 P.M., lights out. The shower room opened at 6:00 P.M., and the students also could use the washing machine that was on the home floor. By 10:00 P.M., students were to have taken care of their hygienic needs, room cleaning chores, and any other type of activity that required them to be outside their individual rooms. After lights out, students were expected to remain in their rooms until the following morning, except for bathroom use and smoke breaks.

During Data Period IV, a typical Saturday provided some changes in the weekly schedule. Breakfast began at 9:00 A.M., permitting the students a later awakening time. However, since the home floor remained open all day, the students could skip breakfast and remain in bed for as long as they desired. Some students often chose to remain in bed all day on Saturday. The cafeteria and the lounge remained open until 10:00 A.M., at which time all the students returned to the home floor. An NTS barber came to the project for the remainder of Saturday morning to give haircuts to those students who wanted and could pay for them. Recreational activities were available from 10:30 A.M. until 12:00 noon, when lunch was served. Student entrance to the cafeteria according to educational grade levels was enforced as it was on weekdays. At 1:00 P.M. the cafeteria closed and students chose between staying in the lounge or returning to the home floor. Both the store and the lounge opened at 1:00 P.M. on Saturday, and students remaining in the lounge were required to pay an entrance fee. An outside recreation schedule ran from 1:30 to 4:30 P.M., depending on weather conditions and staff availability. Dinner was served from 5:00 P.M. to 6:00 P.M. Thereafter, the cafeteria was closed. Saturday evening activities were similar to those during the week with two major exceptions: The educational floor was not opened except for the 7:00 to 9:00 P.M. showing of the CASE II Saturday Night Movie, and the students returned to the home floor at 11:00 P.M., one hour later than during the week. This later lights out schedule was employed on Friday, Saturday, and any night that preceded a holiday.

The schedule for a typical Sunday was basically a free schedule. However, religious services were available during the morning period. Visiting hours were between 1:00 P.M. and 4:00 P.M., and a gym period was scheduled from 6:30 to 8:00 P.M. The students voted for a two-meal schedule on Sunday: 10:30 A.M. and 4:30 P.M. Unlike Monday through Saturday procedure, all students were served on a first-come-first-served basis at both meals.

All legal holidays were observed, and activities on those days followed a Sunday schedule. In addition to special trips taken off site, two parties were held, the first in the Jefferson Hall lounge and the second at a church-sponsored facility in the District of Columbia.

A COMPOSITE STUDENT

In the educational program, more than in any other aspect of CASE operations, the behavior of each student was governed by a series of procedures which were applicable to the entire student population. These procedures were specified in detail for the entire course of the project. There were, however, a number of significant changes made in the procedures during the term of the project. The educational progress of one composite student illustrates these changes made during the year. Admittedly, no one student accurately represents the interaction between the project and the range of students enrolled; the behaviors of other students have been included if they are representative of this interaction and reflect a typical student's activity. In the presentation of this composite student's activities, the actual sequence of project events has been maintained.

Paul, our composite student, was assigned to CASE following his entrance to the National Training School for Boys on April 1, 1966. Paul was sentenced for a crime against property and was given a three-year term. He was a short, slender sixteen-year-old youth from a ghetto neighborhood of a large eastern city. Although his home life was characterized by extreme disorder, and although this was his fifth offense, this was the first time that Paul had been prosecuted in juvenile court. His four previous offenses occurred within a short time span, immediately before the offense for which he was institutionalized. All previous offenses were prosecuted in state criminal courts. He was out on bail at the time of the current offense.

His initial interview with the CASE project director revealed that Paul's early school years were characterized by increasingly frequent friction with teachers. Paul thought that this difficulty was the result of his misunderstanding of verbal instructions. Spanish was spoken in his home; one parent spoke some English. He attended many schools between the first and sixth grades. During the fifth grade, he began to be truant and was expelled in the seventh grade both for truancy and for throwing a chair at a teacher who, he claimed, made insulting remarks against his mother. He was forced to repeat the seventh grade, became increasingly truant during the seventh and eighth grades, and dropped out of school after completing two months of the ninth grade.

During this initial CASE interview, Paul did not express any interest in school work or in any school related activities. He considered mathematics as one academic subject in which he was both interested and able to succeed. He also noted that a knowledge of mathematics was more important than a knowledge of the English language to be able to succeed in any socially acceptable activities on the street. After being instructed in the general nature of the project, Paul willingly bet that he would not be able to maintain the required academic activity and that he would be thrown out of the project within a very short period of time.

In his interview with the CASE educational coordinator, Paul expressed little hope that he could succeed in an academically oriented project. He indicated that he was going to show how really smart he was by "getting everything right on every test," thereby earning enough during the testing period to assure him of sufficient income during the early weeks of his stay in the project. Paul began taking the battery of entrance tests immediately following his one-hour interview with the educational coordinator.

The entrance battery of tests included the Stanford Achievement Test (Form J, advanced), used to assess his general level of academic skill; the Gates Reading Survey, also used as a measure of achievement; and a number of other tests drawn from the instructional materials used in the project and used as diagnostic and placement instruments. The seven subtests of the Stanford Achievement Test, the three parts of the Gates Reading Survey, and the individual tests from the CASE project curriculum were interspersed with a series of short interviews with the educational coordinator. Instructional sessions with other staff members regarding the educational procedures were interspersed during this first week with periods for self-study of orientation material provided by the project.

The results of the Stanford Achievement Test indicated that Paul had between sixth and eighth grade proficiency in arithmetic, social studies, and science skills. His overall proficiency in language-related subtests was lower; his score on the English language usage subtest was below the fifth grade level; his reading scores indicated an ability beyond the eighth grade. The curriculum-based tests showed a similar pattern of abilities. He scored well over 90 per cent on all tests in elementary mathematics, suggesting that he might be able to perform at a ninth or tenth grade level in math. The science-related tests indicated accuracy rates between 35 and 50 per cent on all programed areas. Again, his English language skills were well below par; on no test did he score over 25 per cent accuracy. It appeared that Paul's specific deficiencies in language skills included organizing and verbalizing.

70

General Operation

During an interview with the educational coordinator, Paul described himself as an educational failure. He said that he felt worst about not passing a course in Spanish while he was in high school. He pointed out that Spanish was his native language, and he could not even get that right. On the basis of his entrance testing, Paul was permitted to start working on one of three different programs in each of three curriculum areas: English language, mathematics, and science. Paul was one of the very few students entering CASE II who was not permitted initially to select a program in reading. Because of his relatively high reading scores, his involvement with this curriculum area was delayed.

After his initial selection of three programs, the educational coordinator encouraged Paul to begin working on self-instructional materials in mathematics. Paul was assigned a unit in the program on which he had already demonstrated some initial success. He had scored 70 per cent on its pretest during his entrance testing. Because Paul would be required to read all verbal material concerned with the program, and because he would be required to construct written responses to all questions, he would be gaining practice with English language skills, his weakest area. Like that of all students, Paul's first week of working with the self-instructional curriculum was punctuated by halts, failures, and curiosity about this method of instruction, but his recovery to a pattern of successful self-instructional work was rapid. Within the first three weeks, Paul branched out to take self-instructional programs in the other two subject matter areas, science and English.

After one month in CASE, Paul was promoted to sophomore standing within the project (grades 5, 6, 7). About this same time he began to experience success in the English language programs he was taking, and was one of the first students to enroll in an English rhetoric course scheduled at that time. Shortly thereafter he dropped the course and became one of the first students to use the library during his break time. Conversely, he began to experience difficulty in the testing situation and instigated horseplay in the study area when he was not actively working on his programs.

During school holidays on May 12 and 13, while outside

71

activities were scheduled for all students, he alerted the staff to the escape of two other students. He was warmly but carefully praised for his actions by the staff while incurring the ridicule of many students.

On May 16 an abrupt change in his pattern of horseplay came about. It ceased. This was immediately after the correctional officer was removed from the educational area as a supervisor. Paul did not like this particular correctional officer. Also, at about this time Paul paid for enrollment in a newly-offered math class. He attended only one session.

By June 10, Paul's horseplay had increased and he had received a number of small and large fines. Paul took the regularly scheduled Stanford Achievement Test battery with all the other students. His scores indicated notable progress in science and mathematics but little change in all other areas of the test (language usage, spelling, and social studies). He felt defeated by his lack of progress in these areas and concluded after the scores were posted that he "would never be any damn good with these tests because my English and reading ain't good."

Immediately after the Stanford Achievement Test battery, he began selecting more self-instructional material in reading and English. Because of the increased number of programs he had successfully completed, Paul was promoted to junior status on July 6, three months after his entrance to CASE.

A part of project planning included elimination of hourly wages paid to the students for the time they spent in self-instructional study and classroom activities. On July 7 these hourly wages were terminated and students were paid only for self-instructional study and classwork completed at 90 per cent or better. Along with the majority of students, Paul argued against this change. In fact, he became an organizer and helped lead a student strike the following morning. The strike was resolved, and he returned to work the following day along with all the students. Although the resolution of the problem was accepted by the majority of the students, Paul bombarded the project administration with a series of letters demanding that the staff "respect students' rights."

General Operation

By July 12 he resumed working intensely for long periods of time on English, but he began to request more and more programs in mathematics. On July 20, one of his closest friends was promoted to the junior level (a feat that neither of them thought could occur) and they did an impromptu dance in the study area to express their pleasure. The following day, he balked at new regulations which specified that a student had to complete a unit of program work before he was permitted to change to a different program. All of the students were upset by this additional regulation, but Paul was the most verbal in his protest. Paul's behavioral problems during testing increased dramatically during this time. For expediency, the educational coordinator permitted him to begin a new science program developed to coordinate with the math program that he was experiencing difficulty with. After Paul started the science program, his testing problems decreased markedly. A thorough review of both his behavior and the less dramatic behavior of other students who had worked on this particular math program led the staff to closely review the program. It was found that the math program was faulty and, after revisions were made to it, Paul was put back on the math. He continued working with no difficulty, and his testing room behavior was exemplary.

At about this same time, Paul received an extremely large fine when he was observed reading test answers written on his shirt cuff. In a letter of appeal to the CASE administration he stated: (1) the answers were not the answers to the test he was taking; (2) the shirt was not his; and (3) he wasn't even looking at the answers anyway. The staff was amused by his reasons but gave him the fine. Thereafter, they kept a close watch on his activities in the testing room.

On August 2, immediately following a posted announcement of a program of work release and school release for seniors, Paul submitted a request to be placed on either of the programs. Like all other students who were juniors, he was informed that action on his request would be deferred until he had achieved senior status within the project.

On August 16, Paul was given his third Stanford Achieve-

73

ment Test. Paul had made dramatic increases in English (2.1 grade levels) and math (1.4 grade levels) from his second test administration. There was, however, a notable drop in his science test score. During the first half of the month of August, his social behavior in the educational area did not improve, and he was often awarded small fines for improper language and horseplay. These violations were not serious ones, but their frequency kept the staff consistently sensitive to his actions.

On August 20, he requested an interview with the associate director regarding his lack of social progress as evidenced by frequent horseplay. He recognized that he could not participate in scheduled swimming trips because of his incurred fines. Further, because of these fines, his name had been excluded from the list of students awarded honor status within the project. He admitted that he was unhappy over the consequences of his misbehaviors, of the losses of these special privileges. These were his first acknowledgments to the staff that he was bothered by the results of his own social behavior.

A party and dance was scheduled for August 26 at a church in Washington, D.C. Because a number of girls had been invited by the church pastor, most students were extremely anxious to go. Paul did not attend this social function but stayed at the National Training School. The few students who did stay were supervised by a regular National Training School officer. Paul's vulgar language and horseplay got him into trouble again. Paul was sent to the National Training School's security unit. He was released the following morning but performed no academic activities for the following two days. By the beginning of the following week his educational behaviors had picked up, and he was working in math, English, and social studies. His testing behavior was good.

On September 10, a new chief correctional officer was brought into the project. Paul's social misbehavior was directed against this new officer. In this instance, however, the difficulty appeared to be as much the fault of the officer as of the student. On September 20, Paul chose voluntarily to go on project relief even though he had the money to pay for his room and board. He was the first student to choose relief. He never offered an explanation for this choice, and none was clearly evident to the staff. During this period of time, he maintained his rapid and accurate work on social studies materials, slowed a bit on English language programs, and began to have a difficult time with a new math program he had just started.

On September 30, the project administration was startled by a major disruption. Six students who were watching television one evening escaped by removing a window pane from the television room. Paul was one of these six students. He apparently had second thoughts almost immediately after leaving the building. Upon reaching the street, Paul hailed a patrol car and was taken to a local police station. He returned to the project the following morning but was placed in the National Training School security unit for three days. After his return to the CASE project, he did little or no educational work for almost a week. The following week, however, he resumed his study in both English and math and his work time returned to his normal performance range.

On October 6, a retention testing battery was given to all students. It covered the self-instructional material each student had worked on up to that date. Significantly, Paul evidenced the greatest retention of skills developed in English language and mathematics programs. Most of his English and math tests were completed at 85 per cent accuracy or better. He had completed some of these programs more than five months earlier. On October 13, another scheduled Stanford Achievement Test was given. Paul showed his greatest gains in the social studies, mathematics, and English language usage subtests.

Beginning on October 14, a new system was put into effect for payment of points earned for testing. This new payment schedule entailed payment of 125 per cent of the face value of a test if that test was passed the first time, 100 per cent payment if passed the second time, and 75 per cent payment if passed the third time. With the new test procedures, Paul demonstrated an ability to pass many tests on the first try although formerly he had had to try

75

two and often three times (with corresponding review sessions) before passing a test. This was another dramatic change in Paul's testing behavior.

On October 16—six and one-half months after his entrance to CASE—because of his record of successfully completed programs, Paul was promoted to senior level status (grades 10, 11, 12). Immediately following his receipt of the notice of promotion, Paul paid for and enrolled in a newly opened class in English. This was another marked change in his behavior. He had previously enrolled in a classroom course, but had dropped it after one session. He completed the English class.

On November 1, Paul sought and was granted an interview with the project director. During this interview, he stated a desire to return to high school upon his return to the community. Paul was informed that he would qualify to take the Tests of General Educational Development (a high school equivalency examination). He was pleased to hear of the opportunity but felt that, even if he passed these tests, he wished to return to school full time upon release so that he could complete his final year in high school, in order to be better prepared to pass his state's high school board examinations. He had set a goal for himself, to become "the world's first Puerto Rican architect." He was informed that the staff would do its best to insure that release planning included the opportunity for him to complete high school.

On November 3, Paul experienced another disruption in his school activities. His mother had been transferred from her home in another city to a hospital in Washington, D.C., to undergo exploratory surgery for cancer. Paul was permitted to make a trip to the hospital with one of the part-time CASE staff members, both to relieve his anxiety about his mother and to assist in preparing him for what appeared to be a future parole recommendation. Although he did make the trip, he was not able to wear clothing purchased in the project because all of the money he had made during his educational study had been, as he phrased it, "dribbled away on little junk." He was issued clothing from the National Training School's supply. Despite his embarrassment over his appearance, he went to see his mother. The visit appeared to buoy his spirits considerably, but he missed school for half of the academic day and therefore he did not earn points. The staff member who went with him spoke fluent Spanish and was able to inform Paul's mother of his progress within the project. On the following few days, despite the staff member's good progress report, Paul's performance in the educational program was minimal and his horseplay was more frequent.

By the beginning of the following week, his educational activity returned to normal. He began working on a new and specially prepared geometry program which both he and the staff concluded was in keeping with his desire to become an architect.

On November 7, Paul met with the United States Board of Parole in a regularly scheduled parole review. For this meeting, the CASE staff had prepared a recommendation for parole which emphasized Paul's progress within the project and his apparent ability to effect decisions for appropriate parole status. His repeated but minor acts of horseplay were acknowledged to the Parole Board, but the staff noted that his progress far outweighed his horseplay. It was also indicated that retaining Paul in prison for two more years, even under conditions such as those found in the CASE project, would be detrimental to his overall growth. On November 15, Paul enrolled in a class entitled Jet-Set Science. Previously, he had chosen not to enroll in any science-oriented project. At about this same time, a new demand was placed upon students. All juniors and seniors were required to spell every word correctly on a test answer or receive no credit for that answer. As a direct result of this new rule, Paul's accuracy increased and he appeared to attend more closely to details of the questions.

On November 22, Paul and two other CASE students were administered the Tests of General Educational Development at the National Training School academic school. This high school equivalency examination is given periodically at the NTS. During this administration, three other NTS inmates took the test. When he returned to the project after the test, Paul expressed extreme apprehension about his performance on the test. On November 25, Paul joined a physiology class but dropped it almost immediately because he did not get along with the instructor. That same day, he indicated to the educational coordinator that he did not wish to work further on the mathematics programs he was taking. A supplemental note from the correctional officer indicated that Paul had received a letter from his mother (who was still in the hospital) and that she was extremely worried about the fact that she had gotten no reports on the results of the exploratory surgery. He later admitted to the educational coordinator that his concern about his mother led him to feel depressed about "just about everything in this whole damn place." On December 4, he began to work again on programs in the English language curriculum. However, he expressed anxiety about the possible results of his scores on the Tests of General Educational Development. He also began to work on math programs that he had dropped a few days earlier.

On December 6, Paul was informed that he had successfully passed the Tests of General Educational Development. His percentile ranking among all United States students on the five tests which comprised the General Educational Development battery averaged 50 per cent. His highest percentile rank for any one test was in general mathematical ability—52 per cent. His lowest percentile rank was in correctness and effectiveness of expression—24 per cent. Paul was elated at these results. The following day, he submitted a written request for a position in the work release program. He was informed by the staff that his general behavior would have to improve before he could take a half-time work position, and that he would have to remain in the educational program working full-time until his general behavior did improve. He was miffed at this response, but admitted to the educational coordinator that it was in keeping with his overall goal of returning to high school. Following this exchange, his behavior within the educational program became model. From this time until December 16, Paul worked steadily on English, math, and social studies. Thereafter, Paul became obnoxious with the educational staff during only one brief period in the testing room.

On December 16, the Army Revised Beta examination (an

IQ test) was given to all CASE students. Paul's score had increased twenty points since his initial entry testing. Also on December 16, Paul was informed by the CASE caseworker that the United States Board of Parole had favorably reviewed the recommendation of the staff and that he had been granted parole effective February 20, 1967. He was also informed that his parole had been delayed from an original date, December 20, because of his involvement in the escape two and one-half months earlier.

On December 19, Paul was involved in a minor altercation in the educational area. At this time, a number of National Training School teachers were participating in the project for on-the-job training. These were the teachers who were to be working in the new educational programs—modeled after CASE—at the NTS. During a program checking session with two of these trainees, Paul asserted that they misunderstood both the intent and function of specific procedures about which they were counseling him. He proceeded to clarify for the trainees what he considered were the procedures, noting that, "I know, 'cause I've been in trouble with them enough already."

Paul's Christmas was bleak. He had received no correspondence or gifts from his family. His educational performance during this time dropped off to practically nothing. On December 26, Paul was informed that his mother's surgery had indicated no trace of malignancy. Paul was extremely relieved. By December 28, Paul had earned a half-time job within the work release program. This job was during the normal morning study hours and he was assigned the duties of a staff clerical worker. He remained half time in the educational program during the afternoons.

During the time between the end of December and February 20, Paul was not involved in any obvious disruptions or incidents. Just before he left on parole, he was given a final battery of educational examinations. On the Stanford Achievement Test, Paul's academic growth from April to January was quite dramatic. In paragraph meaning, his score increased one and three-quarter grades; in spelling, one and one-quarter grades; in language usage, four and three-quarter grades; in arithmetic reasoning, two and

79

one-quarter grades; in arithmetic computation, three and one-quarter grades; in social studies, two and one-half grades; and in science his scores remained about the same.

On February 20, 1967, Paul left the CASE project. His destination: home, with his father; a part-time job in a local work project; and full-time enrollment in a local high school.

Chapter 5

Cultural and
Interpersonal Results

*O*ften, because of our fractionated professional and civic approach to problem solving, design solutions are offered without consideration of all the factors that impinge upon a behavioral event. Putting up benches and carefully designed waste containers in a park does not ensure their use. Foremost among the variables that have been found effective in governing behavior are the consequences that are attached to it.

CONSEQUENCES AND ENVIRONMENTAL DESIGN

In the field of environmental design, architects and planners usually have no control over the variables governing behavior when they redesign the environment. This lack of control was exemplified in major cities immediately after World War II. In the name of urban renewal, slum dwellings were demolished and new high rise apartment communities were erected in their place. Shortly after occupancy, the hallways, lobbies, and other group spaces began to change. A good example was a housing project in Chicago, Illinois. There, the freshly painted wall surfaces became a challenge to the occupants. Graffiti specialists, pornographic artists, and angry youth attacked the walls like skilled painters at a fresh canvas. Soon the new environment displayed the same visual and olfactory signals as had the old housing areas. Human behavior can be stimulated by visual and environmental cues. However, the direction, whether constructive or not, depends upon the consequences. With no aversive consequences for antisocial behavior, the destructive activity continued. Further, if such behavior was to be terminated, effective alternatives as well as aversive control would have had to be employed. Unfortunately, alternatives for the visual and physical abasement of those properties were not used. In a few years, there was little to distinguish some of the new environments from the old ones.

The CASE project needed to provide an environment in which its students would have space for work, rest, and recreation. Funds were not available for a new structure, and so Jefferson Hall was selected for redesign. Few structural alterations were made. The most notable modification was that all the walls and ceilings were painted a stark white. The NTS painting crews commented that those white walls would soon look like American public bathrooms —covered with prose and graffiti. Unlike the housing projects, CASE constructed both an environment and a series of behavioral programs for its captive audience. CASE provided systems of consequences for both desirable and undesirable behavior. It also offered a variety of alternate activities from which the students could choose. Many of these were incompatible with defacement and abuse of property.

The CASE environment was designed with both behavioral alternatives and wide ranging consequences geared to develop, reinforce, and maintain acceptable and positive academic and social behaviors. The staff found that the removal or rescheduling of certain environmental cues (the pool table, television sets, pinball machines, library facilities, and so on) and the lack of reinforcement for antisocial behavior made abusive behavior nearly nonexistent. The students' treatment of their environmental space and of both project and private property was exemplary.

During the term of the project, certain student attitudes appeared to undergo dramatic changes. Each student began his stay by spending most of his time and money obtaining consumable items related to his daily room and meal needs. In time, this pattern changed and the student began purchasing more durable items. These new purchases included clothing for himself, gifts for relatives and friends, and goods or food for parents and other relatives. The students also placed money in trust with the CASE bank. This behavioral trend represented a measurable shift toward acceptable middle class values.

During the students' orientations into the CASE community, the correctional staff recorded behavior that the uninitiated would consider bizarre. This behavior was labeled the "bathroom syndrome." During their first few nights at CASE, the students slept very little and frequently stopped on their way to or from the bathroom to talk with the correctional officer. They talked about their backgrounds and interests and why they were incarcerated, and the officer talked to the students about the requirements and benefits of the CASE program. Entering CASE with a history of confinement at other institutions (some from as many as four), these students were concerned about their physical security. They seemed to be checking out the system. Going to the bathroom at night produced many opportunities for talking with the correctional officer. On the average students took between two and three nights, but never more than six, before they were able to evaluate the security system in the new environment and sleep through the night. The bathroom syndrome disappeared. Although this behavior is not uncommon in prisons, the National Training School considered this inappropriate, and inmates were subjected to ridicule if it occurred too frequently. In CASE, the night officers were encouraged to openly discuss all issues and specifically to point out the security systems designed to assure the privacy and dignity of each individual. Each student's adaptation to the CASE environment was considered crucial and was handled accordingly.

A major environmental adjustment for most students was the racial one. In CASE all students, blacks and whites, were required to live together. For the white rural southerner, being required to live with aggressive northern blacks proved disturbing. Some of the blacks had far more education than the white students. As CASE opened, only one-fourth of the students were black. The remaining students were white and evenly divided between urban and rural backgrounds. Most were from the South. One group of southern whites created a clique and referred to themselves as the "Rebs." These students would get together in the lounge or on the home floor and discuss what was common to them from their past. They recreated local histories complete with social customs, favorite popular music, and intriguing food selections. At first the Rebs were the dominant group in the project, and the black students avoided the pervasive presence of this group.

The balance between black and white students changed within the first two months of the project. CASE asked for and was assigned six black students at one time. This shifted the racial complement radically. For the next few weeks, the staff experienced strong pressure on the system. Vocal outbursts, verbal antagonism, and anger increased daily. One series of incidents centered around two black students who openly advocated black racial superiority. These students and their views were met with aggressive hostility from a number of white southerners, particularly the Rebs. Tensions mounted, and incidents between these two students and the whites increased, but no physical violence resulted. The tension was finally resolved, although not to the complete satisfaction of the staff, when these two black students escaped from the NTS. As a consequence of these racial and social activities, new subcomponents of the management system were put into practice.

The Committee for Student Affairs, the students, the staff, and the elected student government cooperated in the operation of CASE. The established behavioral organization was maintained as an open system. CASE encouraged frequent and open discussions, hid nothing from the students, and (in what appeared to be a short period of time) a new sense of community was felt. The students were "mixing it up." They learned what most people must come to learn—the loss of fear through familiarization. They also learned that one can have different friends for different reasons and in different activities. The southerners kept their identity as southerners; the blacks kept theirs as blacks. However, they all joined in new social groupings when they enrolled in classes, when they played games of baseball and pool, and when they engaged in outside social functions. They learned to enjoy each other's differences, yet they maintained their own identities. In these days, when the ability of democratic institutions to support racial, economic, or social differences is being questioned, the CASE project provided a measured demonstration that such a system does work when it remains honest and consistent. It succeeds when it fulfills its commitment and delivers the choices and payoffs it promises.

In a society that values private ownership, citizens learn to maintain and enjoy the results of their labors. Many of the students had never had a private bedroom or work area and had never experienced either the pride of ownership or the sharing of work in a joint venture. The offices that were provided and in which the students spent at least twenty-five hours each week doing educational work were barren in the beginning. However, before long these offices became visually exciting and personal. The students bought materials from the store, made drawings, collected cutouts from magazines, and made their offices personal showplaces. The "keeping up with the Joneses" phenomenon was eminently visible in CASE.

The students accentuated their individuality even more on the home floor in their private rooms. The first decoration was usually a *Playboy* pinup. Some staff believed that the students pinned up nudes to stimulate masturbation. Others felt that this was a student's way of telling the others that he was a man, that he liked looking at pictures of nude women. Soon each room became an extremely personal homelike environment. Most students built shelves, painted walls, bought rugs for the floors, and decorated their rooms with a variety of eye-catching articles. The students not only decorated their rooms but expressed a pride of ownership which was reinforced by comments and bonuses from the staff. The interior decorating activity on the home floor was sustained for the full term of the program, even after the staff stopped giving point bonuses for such activity about midway through the program. Although the dispensation of point bonuses for this activity encouraged students to decorate their own rooms, the most effective controls for maintaining this behavior were exercised by the students' peers. Here, social reinforcement clearly maintained room decoration and other appropriate social skills. Students began to meet regularly in certain private rooms and students vied for the attention of this roving group of visitors. Concurrently, walls were not defaced, garbage was not dumped, property was not destroyed, and rooms were scrupulously maintained.

Pride of ownership and of community care was available through the CASE economy because the students could purchase materials, gather supplies, apportion time, and develop plans for the development of personal environments. During the entire program, there were no instances of major destruction to general CASE property, except in the case of one youngster who in a rage tore down a small screening wall near one private room. Destruction of a student's personal property occurred only once.

The lounge provided another example of how the CASE program fostered appropriate social behavior. The lounge was the one area within the project where the students could engage in a full range of social activities. By the end of the third project month, the lounge had become a garbage dump. Refuse was not being put into wastebaskets. Candy wrappers and bottles were left on tables, and cigarette butts and other litter were thrown on the floor. It had become difficult for the storekeeper to keep the lounge clean.

The storekeeper complained. The Committee for Student Affairs posted a higher hourly charge for the lounge. Students grumbled and complained, asking, "What's with the higher prices? We're not getting anything extra for it." The Committee for Student Affairs replied, "Because it is costing us more money to clean and maintain the lounge, we are forced, like any good local government, to tax you—to increase the lounge rate—to help pay for the additional cleaning services." This extra funding was used to hire two student workers for daily lounge clean-up duties beyond those handled by the janitorial staff. The students were told that if undeposited trash decreased, the lounge rate would be reduced to its previous level. The students got the message. Within two weeks the level of trash accumulation decreased, and the lounge rate was reduced.

CASE students also worked for their community (when the community reciprocally worked for them) by reshaping and maintaining the recreational areas and grounds surrounding Jefferson Hall. Although Jefferson Hall was on the boundary of NTS property and was surrounded by trees, lawns, and a variety of playing fields, these areas were poorly maintained. CASE students received outdoor recreation privileges throughout the year. Because they could entertain their families outdoors during visiting hours, they expressed concern for the appearance of the grounds surrounding Jefferson Hall. Students requested and received permission to reseed bare spots in the lawn. They also refurbished worn and damaged equipment and constructed a new game area. CASE purchased some groundkeeping equipment and borrowed some from the National Training School. Throughout the spring and summer, the CASE students planted and tended grass and flowers, developed attractive arrangements of outdoor furniture, constructed a new horseshoe pit and football playing field, and outfitted the basketball court with new hoops, nets, and all court markings. The students told the staff that they began and continued these activities because there was a direct payoff. They were able to entertain their family, friends, and visiting students from the NTS in pleasant surroundings.

ADOLESCENT SEXUAL BEHAVIORS

The dramatic hormonal changes and rapid physical development that adolescents experience between the ages of eleven and sixteen frequently cause concern in parents. The observable physical development and corresponding social behavior changes are often seen as unhappy deviations from childhood. Some adults view the more obvious social sexual development as bad behavior and make a variety of attempts to suppress it. Confinement in a penal environment amplifies both the demonstrated behavior and the means of control. For example, the NTS made a practice of not hiring young attractive women for its training staff. Photographs of unclad parts of the female body in magazines such as *Life, Look,* and *Time* were removed before the magazines were distributed to NTS magazine racks. Articles about the South Sea Islands or African natives which showed nude figures were censored. NTS staff screened weekend entertainment movies and showed none that suggested sexual interaction with women or that provided any stimulating content.

In the traditional penal institution where the individual inmate has no privacy for sleeping or showering and certain normal sexual behaviors are restricted, an institutional form of sexual maturation is emphasized. Masturbation can either be ridiculed or punished by the correctional staff, because it must always take place in a group situation. Exhibitionism is often practiced by the inmates, and institutions such as NTS record frequent incidents of homosexual rape. Young men were sexually assaulted at NTS in the stairwells of cottages on their way to bed or in the bathroom during the evening recreation hours. Sexual abuse occurred in the gang showers where correctional officers were not able to maintain visual control. Cases have been reported in which officers watched youngsters being sexually assaulted and reported the incidents only after the abused students complained to a higher administrator. Whether such activities lead to a misdirection of sexual behavior following release from such an institution may be a moot question; however, these activities in themselves are compelling reasons for abolition of environmental and social controls that promote them.

The CASE students exhibited normal sexual development. However, the approach taken by the CASE program was significantly different from that in practice in the remainder of the NTS. Young, attractive women were sought and hired for the training staff. The students were permitted to look at pictures of the unclad female body if they purchased magazines in the store and read them on the home floor. Privacy was provided by their rooms and shower arrangements, as mentioned before. At all times the CASE project attempted to develop social and environmental controls and encourage behaviors which the students could experience in their own communities. These students were becoming men and they were treated as such. (Some of the students had long since established that claim by fathering children out of wedlock.) They were encouraged to date young women while on leave from the project. They could earn a one-day or weekend pass to town by maintaining their academic and social behavior in the project. Through these means and social events organized by CASE they could experience normal contact with members of the opposite sex.

Two incidents from the history of CASE will help illuminate the problems created by herding youngsters into a penal environment. After the chief chaplain of the Federal Bureau of Prisons visited CASE, the CASE director received a call from the director of the Bureau. The chief chaplain had informed the Bureau director that during his entire professional career at the Bureau he had "never witnessed such vulgarity and filth as that seen on the home floor of Jefferson Hall." The chaplain was shocked by the pinups of nude women in the students' rooms, the unmade beds, and the dust. The CASE director replied to the director of the Bureau that looking at women and exhibiting special interest in women was being reinforced as good and normal behavior, and that the students were not at that time being reinforced for making their beds and dusting their rooms. The program for promoting student housekeeping was not scheduled to start in CASE until later. Tactfully, four points were made to clarify this issue: (1) CASE was concerned with developing student self-control, not with maintaining forced discipline which was not likely to be maintained in the real world. (2) The aversive procedures generally used in prisons to maintain cleanliness and order are not necessarily useful in the rehabilitation of inmates. (3) Traditional penal methods appeared counterproductive in developing adolescents who are prepared to live in a heterosexual democratic society. (4) By punishing normal behavior concerning women and sex (while enforcing social curiosities such as having naked students walk in a group up two flights of steps to their dormitories), the NTS was fostering homosexuality and encouraging homosexual rape. CASE was never again bothered by either the chaplain or the director of the Bureau about this part of the program.

The problems of homosexuality within an insular and all

male social system are well known. Although such sexual deviance is exhibited in boys' schools and the army, a prison potentiates it within a more volatile situation. The CASE program was designed to reduce homosexual incidents. By encouraging privacy, by bringing women into the program as staff members, and by permitting the young men to read a variety of magazines and engage in normal dating behaviors CASE created a more normal adolescent environment than was then available at the National Training School.

An ample amount of horseplay—wrestling, friendly hanging on, and dancing—was seen within Jefferson Hall, but no overt homosexual activities appeared until an eighteen year old white male exhibiting homosexual dress and behavior during his initial interview was brought into the program. This student's entering behavior indicated that CASE was about to have its first homosexual problem. The correctional staff suggested that this young man should be removed from the project and put into isolation or that heavy punishment should be delivered just as soon as he made his first obvious homosexual move. This was the traditional way the NTS handled aggressive homosexual activity. The CASE staff decided to wait and see.

Within three weeks' time, this student had become fast friends with three of the younger white males. These students soon displayed a new dress style, exposed their bodies by tying up their shirts around their stomachs, wore their hair in a longer and distinctive style, and created a family situation in which the new student acted alternately as the father and mother of the group. One day the CASE director received a call from the home floor officer, who informed him that this student had been seen kissing one of his followers. These two students were brought to the director's office and asked to respond to the officer's report. The conversation was as follows: *Director:* "Officer Short just called me to say that you guys were kissing and tonguing each other in the ear. Was that true?" *Student:* "Yes, we love each other and we want to get married. You said that we could have whatever we want since this is a democratic society, so we would like to rent two rooms together, break down the wall, and make our own home." *Director:* "I have no objection to your needs. However, you know as I do that a lot of guys would like to have their girl friends here. Although you guys want each other, they would prefer women. You're quite right in saying that this is a democratic society, and if I give you the opportunity to sleep together I must give the same option to the guys who want their women. However, the federal prison rules state that I cannot permit women on to the home floor, certainly not to spend the night. I must, therefore, turn down your request."

The students grumbled but agreed that these arrangements could not be made in CASE. The director prided himself on the fact that he had resolved a problem. However, it soon became apparent that no real contribution had been made to a final solution. That same evening the two students broke out of Jefferson Hall, by removing panes of glass from the television room windows, and escaped.

The Committee for Student Affairs held a special meeting. Five principles were outlined for the handling of future incidents of this kind. Such students were to be informed that there are some states in which homosexual activity between consenting adults is permitted, but only within the privacy of their own home. CASE was to inform these students of ways of securing privacy for such a relationship. If such students wished to engage in a relationship of this kind, they should work for weekend passes together and take a room at a hotel or the YMCA where, in privacy, they could handle their sexual needs in any manner they saw fit. CASE was not to attempt to moralize or pass judgment upon their behavior but only to point out the legal situation. And CASE was to offer some formal counseling service for students who demonstrated by their behavior that they were in need of human love and affection. Eventually, the aggressive homosexual was captured and returned to the project. He regained full student status in the program and was assigned to a psychiatric counselor.

ADJUSTMENT TO RELEASE

Institutionalization is a behavioral condition developed by removing an individual from all the normal choices and reinforcing properties that are available to him in a free and democratic society. Often mental and penal institutions help shape the institutionalization, creating maladaptive behaviors that are inimical to returning the individual to his previous environment in the outside world. One of the questions most frequently asked by inmates is "Will people accept me?" The problem of phasing an individual back to his local community and family was undertaken by a section of the Committee for Student Affairs. This group comprised the executive director, the CASE worker, and two other workers of the research staff. Their specific duties included the management of programs designed to facilitate the student's return to society. More students experienced difficulties in making this adjustment than made it readily. A dramatic incident of poor adjustment was the case of Roger.

This student was raised in a small southern town. CASE reports indicated a turbulent home life, disrupted childhood, and unfavorable reaction to all types of school situations. His mother had taken many lovers, his siblings lived with a variety of relatives, and his natural father had left the home to live in an abandoned automobile and run a junk yard. When Roger entered CASE, his mother had been married and divorced three times. During his stay in the program, she married a fourth time and moved to California. It appeared from their correspondence that the mother had made little effort to encourage Roger to live with her and her new husband after his release. During his initial parole hearings, Roger spoke out clearly in favor of his parole. However, when the parole grant was authorized, his behavior changed dramatically.

He became abusive toward the training staff. Teachers reported that his work rate decreased and that he had become a general nuisance to other students on the educational floor. The staff talked with Roger to determine the reason for his changed behavior. He pointed out that he was "just getting back at CASE" and that he was "glad to get out of this damned place." His behavior became more obnoxious and eventually included cursing at correctional staff, fighting with other students, and defacing private property of other students (he represented the exceptional case described earlier). Eventually Roger was called to a meeting of the Committee for Student Affairs to account for his actions. Both staff and other students agreed that Roger was exhibiting a high level of "let's stay here" behavior and that he was convinced his mother did not want him at her home. After three weeks, his mother was contacted by telephone. By this time, Roger's behavior had deteriorated. He damaged a divider partition on the home floor, cursed and swore at all staff, and behaved in what appeared to be an irrational manner. Brought before the Committee for Student Affairs again, Roger said that he was certain CASE would "lock him in solitary." He said, "I guess you're going to get my parole turned down." He was informed by the staff, "On the contrary, we recognize that you are upset about going home and we would like to assist you in getting there." At this point, Roger sprang from his chair, began cursing and making vulgar gestures at the staff, pushed his way out of the office, and ran to the home floor.

That evening, during a staff meeting, the director received an emergency call from the home floor officer. Roger had slashed his wrists with a razor blade and locked himself in a closet. Within a half hour the student was hospitalized and under sedation. He had given the project the biggest "let's stay here" signal yet. By the end of Roger's brief hospitalization, the CASE staff had made contact with his mother and had devised a plan to make his transition to parole easier. Roger was to call his mother by telephone twice weekly for four weeks (a nominal fee schedule had been established); following his return from the hospital and after four weeks of twice weekly telephone calls, he was to be given a ten day leave and sent home; and upon his return (if he still felt that he did not want to live at his mother's new home) CASE would renegotiate a parole plan for him with the parole board. The CASE staff had instructed his mother on how she was to behave during the telephone conversations. She assured the staff that both she and her new husband wanted Roger to live with them.

The telephone calls resulted in a new understanding between Roger and his mother. Consequently, Roger spent his ten day vacation at his mother's home, and upon his return he said that he was looking forward to going home. He also indicated that California was great and that his new stepfather seemed to be a reasonable guy. Between the time of his return and his release, he was a diligent and cooperative student. He made plans, he worked hard, and all the destructive behavior disappeared. Within another month, Roger left the CASE project for California.

LETTER WRITING AND VISITS

Policy of the Federal Bureau of Prisons permitted inmates to write letters only to their families (including uncles, aunts, and cousins). This policy tended to restrict the volume of letter writing and to foster lying. The most logical course of action open to an NTS student was to list all girl friends and buddies as cousins. The CASE director discussed this situation with the superintendent of the National Training School and requested permission to have an open mail policy for all CASE students. Eventually permission was granted. Months later, its virtues became apparent to the National Training School. The NTS policy was changed to match that of CASE.

National Training School policy for visitors was similar to that for letter writing—only immediate family could visit and only for a two hour period (from 2:00 to 4:00 o'clock on Sunday afternoons in the Protestant chapel). Emergency visits related to sickness or death in the family were assigned to the front hall of the administration building. CASE requested the same kind of open policy for visiting as had been established for letter writing. The doors of Jefferson Hall were open from 1:00 to 4:00 P.M. each Sunday. The students met their visitors out on the porches, on the front grounds, or in the lounge or dining room.

Although visitors could not bring in or buy anything for the student except at Christmas or for birthdays, the student could use his points to buy a variety of items for his visitors. The student could shoot a game of pool with his father, invite his friends or his family to dinner by prearrangement with the cook, or purchase snacks or gift items in the store for his brothers, sisters, or friends. The number of visitors to CASE was large and disproportionate to the num-

94

ber that visited other National Training School students. Visitors came well dressed, and although they mixed freely with the CASE students, they caused no incidents of friction, violence, or smuggling. Introduction of cousins, sisters, and girl friends to other CASE students became common events.

The attitudes of parents visiting their sons in CASE were influenced by these rules. A mother or father who visited NTS always felt it was important to bring something for the child—some special food or a gift. Parents who were unable to supply these gifts tended not to come often. When CASE established the rule that no visitor could bring gifts, but that conversely the student could buy things for his visitors, the entire approach and attitude of the parent toward the child changed. The following statement by a CASE mother sums up this new attitude:

For years I have always had to do something for him. This is his third time in. He has always brought me trouble, cost me money. I've had to pay lawyers' fees; nothing but trouble he caused me. I work very hard and I have very little money. He has never brought a thing into the house. Now for the first time, he does things for me. He brought me a gift for Mother's Day, he sends home money for food, and I can have dinner with him on Sunday, and like a gentleman, he pays for it. I am very thankful that he was able to get into this project because he has a sense of pride in buying things for me and he also feels good about working for it. My son has learned to take care of himself, and he looks like he may be able to take care of me and his sister when he gets out.

ROLE OF CHAPLAINS

The chaplains' roles at the NTS had been specified long before the CASE project began. They were expected to conduct Sunday services and choir practice, to help in case of family illness or the death of a parent, and to distribute gifts for Christmas and Easter. The CASE program made a direct effort to involve both the Protestant and the Catholic chaplains more directly in the training activities. As a direct result of receiving a recorded evening conversation between two CASE students, the CASE director called the chaplains together. He reported the students' conversation from a midnight smoke break. One of the students had said, "Hey, what's your God like?" The other replied, "I don't know, I'm a Protestant. I haven't seen my God." Again, the first student, "I'm a Catholic and I don't know what my God looks like either." The discussion raised basic questions. Did they both have the same God? If not, how many Gods are there?

The CASE director told the chaplains that he did not think they were serving the best interests of the students, although they were undoubtedly fulfilling their particular church responsibilities. Between them, the chaplains agreed to participate in the educational program of the CASE project. The Protestant chaplain designed a new course in American history and arranged to have lunch three days a week with the students in the CASE cafeteria. Working with two NTS teachers, he developed a programed course instructing his students on how the need for religious freedom in Europe had created the movement to America, on the development of the Reformation, on the problems within the Church of England, and on the break with Rome. The chaplain became a productive teacher rather than a Sunday visitor and sermonizer. The Catholic chaplain felt that he could serve best as a counselor, and he dropped in occasionally to talk with one or more students. He also sent two Catholic brothers to participate with the students in their evening activities. They played ball and became part of the social structure during the evenings and on weekends. The Catholic chaplain also wanted all Catholic boys fram CASE to go to his catechism class on Sundays. The director agreed to permit the students this time out provided they paid for such instruction. Any student could register and pay a fee just as for any other CASE class. At first the chaplain was incensed at placing a money value on everything, and a three week dialogue ensued. The CASE director pointed out that the church is supported by money. These future citizens should learn that they must support both the church of their choice and their country with funds as well as other forms of support. The director indicated that the money collected could be donated to the chaplain's favorite charity, but that each student had to pay each week for the catechism class. Eventually the chaplain conceded and sent one of the brothers to post an announcement for the class. Much to the chaplain's surprise, more Protestants than Catholics registered for the classes.

The CASE library was developed in a series of small steps. In the beginning, the facility was managed as a combination lending library and social center. It was monitored by a young black law student and was open during the evenings and on weekends. As the result of a number of managerial problems, a new classroom-library was created. The library became less of a social center and incorporated more study assistance. Students were permitted to take out books for their friends. One student paid the fixed entrance fee and took out books for any number of his friends. However, the CASE staff recognized that neither of these approaches to establishing a library supported reading behavior in proportion to the number of librarian hours required and the large scale record keeping created. Because the major objective of a well-stocked library should be to ensure that books are read, changes were instituted.

The administration informed the student government that students would be permitted to buy a series of pocketbooks for the program and that CASE would pay the bill. A bookmobile (for sales) was brought to the project and the students selected as many books as the original funding estimate allowed. The inside cover of each book was stamped with the notation "Selected for the CASE Project by student ———," and the purchasing student's name was inserted. Concurrently, CASE purchased a series of wire book racks, the same type that are used for displaying and selling paperback books. The racks were placed in the bathrooms (still considered by many Americans as the only decently lighted place for reading), on the home floor, in the dining room, in the lounge, and in the academic free bench area. A time came when there were more books in students' pockets and in their rooms than there were on the book racks. When the racks emptied, a notice was posted asking students to exchange or replace the books. The system appeared effective in maintaining the desired reading behaviors. Over the entire term of the project, few books were destroyed or mutilated, and most of the original purchases (all paperbacks) survived through almost one year's use. There was no significant decrease in the number of students who used the library. However, few books were ever checked out of the library after the large scale purchase of paperback books. The library eventually became more of an evening study center and the staff in the library began to spend their time assisting students in working through program instructional and traditional study materials.

Historically, man's food preferences have been the result of his environment and of his religious and social mores. The excitement the gourmet experiences from a variety of food tastes and smells has been made available to many people who share the amenities of large metropolitan areas. World travelers have added new foods to their list of the beneficial experiences of visiting new cultures. The young men confined at the National Training School had an extremely limited range of preferred foods. Their food selections were governed by past financial limitations, regional restrictions, and idiosyncratic responses to childhood and adolescent eating experiences. The southern white students preferred a variety of cooked greens (mustard greens, kale, turnip greens), a limited set of starchy foods (blackeyed peas, corn meal, rice, grits), and a limited selection of proteins (barbecued pork, fat back, fried chicken). The black students from the ghettos of Washington seemed to prefer a similar variety of cooked greens; however, their preferences for starchy food included more bread, potatoes, and noodles, while their preferences in protein foods were barbecued ribs, barbecued chicken, chicken wings, scrapple, and sausage. All the students liked hamburgers, hot dogs, French fries, and milk shakes. Foods considered snacks by the majority of the population had broken down regional barriers. With few exceptions, CASE students avoided such healthful foods as fruits and leafy vegetables.

When the CASE food service was changed from a scheduled

menu plan to an open cafeteria plan, the individual's choice of foods became dependent on selection and on his ability to pay. This change made it possible to broaden the students' food selection and preference palate. One of the devices used most was the manipulation of food prices. The new CASE cook devised a plan to shape the students' food selections. Initially, the cook gave away all salad makings, including lettuce, tomatoes, and a range of dressings (lettuce was one food that few of the students had eaten up to that point). Prices were also reduced on foods such as steak rolls, shrimp, fish filets, and liver. Mexican, Chinese, and Italian dinners were displayed at attractive minimal rates. Large scale reductions were given to vegetables that students had previously avoided, such as asparagus, Brussels sprouts, and French beans. Concurrently, the cook increased the price of certain foods that were considered desirable, such as hamburgers, hot dogs, and French fries. Many students who wanted to conserve some of their funds during the week tended to try a new food simply because of its low price. Before long, students were asking for the reintroduction of a previously undesirable set of menu choices.

The food program at the National Training School offered no choices but acceptance or refusal of an item. Further, the NTS students ate their meals in an army-style mess hall. They went through a serving line and their food was placed on metal serving trays. Spoons were the only items acceptable as cutlery at the NTS dining hall. In CASE the students chose their own foods and ate on china with knives, forks, and spoons, making it possible for them to learn how to use the utensils. The students selected the group they wished to join at mealtime. Because the staff ate with the students, the students watched how and when the staff used the utensils. This kind of training, the modeling after adults, produced table manners. Occasionally a student would ask a staff member, "Is it right to pick up the chicken with your fingers?" or "How do you cut this thing, anyway?" There was no doubt that the civil behaviors required in public eating were not a part of the CASE students' existing repertoire when they entered the program. The cafeteria was designed like a traditional restaurant with menus, flowers on the tables, and tablecloths. Socialization with adults in the cafeteria was useful in helping to shape acceptable social eating skills.

The CASE students drank so much milk that their consumption eventually presented the project with a financial problem. At the NTS, students were permitted one glass of milk a day. Under the CASE system, the students could drink as much milk as they could afford to pay for. Not wishing to remove the availability of milk and unable to continue funding large scale consumption, the cook began offering other choices of beverages while concurrently increasing the price of milk from ten to fifteen cents for a large glass. Beverages such as cocoa (water-based) and fruit juice drinks (also water-based) were offered during most meals. The CASE students continued to drink large quantities of milk but quenched their thirst with other liquids.

Although no physiological documentation was made, this new food program appeared to produce an extremely healthy and lively group of students. The CASE staff felt that CASE students even looked different from other NTS students. Some staff members commented that CASE students did not have the prison pallor typical of an inmate. Although there were no restrictions on how much food a student could eat, there was only one case of obesity, and that student had the problem when he entered the program.

PHYSICAL HEALTH

Sick call is generally considered an appropriate way of gold-bricking and getting away from the daily routine. Each morning at the NTS hospital, the students lined up waiting for headache powders, antiseptic for scratches, or medicinal balms for a variety of nondescript ailments. Their behavioral statement was quite clear. It seemed far wiser to waste an hour or more at the clinic than to scrub floors, shovel coal, or perform other aversive tasks.

CASE permitted a sick call at 7:30 A.M. It was rarely used. One day, the assistant director saw one of the students holding his jaw in obvious pain. Some prodding revealed that the student had a severe toothache. The student said that he had not gone to the dentist because he felt that he would have to waste an entire morning waiting for treatment and would lose almost half a day's pay.

Cultural and Interpersonal Results

Here was a basic deficiency in the CASE economic system. A new sick leave policy was instituted. For every full month of active work (of more than twenty-five paid hours per week) the CASE corporation gave each student one-half day sick leave with pay. If the student did not use his accumulated sick leave, he could convert all unused sick leave into regular leave at the rate of one-half day of leave for every whole day of sick leave accrued. This small adjustment in the CASE economic system enabled students to get proper medical care without losing income.

During the project year, there was only one group medical problem. One night more than half the students experienced diarrhea because a kitchen assistant had forgotten to rinse the dishwasher soap out of a cooking pot before it was reused. Surprisingly, there were no major outbreaks of colds, flu, or other communicable diseases. For a confined population, there was an unusual degree of good health.

A few unique medical events illustrate student behavior and interaction with CASE and NTS staff. One incident involved a young black student, Leroy. This youth had had an eczema on his face when he arrived at CASE. After a few weeks, Leroy went on sick call to the hospital. He was told by the medical staff that there was nothing wrong—he should just wash his face. A few weeks later the condition had worsened, and Leroy's skin was flaking off in large patches. Again, he went to sick call. In fact, he was sent to the hospital with one of the CASE correctional staff late in the evening. An hour later he returned to CASE and called the medic a racist. A check with the correctional officer proved Leroy's allegation to be true. The medic had ridiculed him, had called him "old elephant skin," and had made derogatory remarks about both his race and his physical fitness. The situation was brought to the attention of the NTS superintendent. A series of problems which had been fostered by this one member of the medical staff for years were uncovered. This medical officer systematically discriminated against black students. This officer was never released from the NTS, but he was sternly reprimanded by his superiors. Because Leroy was unable to get proper treatment at the NTS, CASE made arrangements for him to be examined by a dermatologist in Washington,

D.C. CASE agreed to pay half of the fee if Leroy would pay the balance. He agreed and went to the private dermatologist. After two visits and a series of tests, the dermatologist discovered that Leroy was allergic to wool and to the blankets and other woolen materials which NTS distributed. Leroy then bought—with his own earnings—new dacron blankets, a new pillow, and sweaters made of orlon. In less than two weeks his facial condition had cleared and his disposition changed. Both were extremely bright.

The second case concerned Sam. He had a deformed nose and muscle distortions about his mouth resulting from a fight he had had when a child. Sam was very conscious of his features. When he talked, it looked as if he was snarling. On first meeting him, people felt he was quite aggressive. In fact, he was mild mannered. After a series of discussions with Sam, CASE recommended that he undergo corrective cosmetic surgery. Again, CASE agreed to pay one-half of the cost if Sam would pay the balance. Although the surgery did not completely correct these physical defects, a cosmetically reshaped nose helped produce a pleasanter face and a correspondingly pleasanter outlook on life.

Another student, Kirk, was embarrassed over some home-made tattoos he had received in a South Carolina jail. His embarrassment increased in front of the female staff. Although it is common practice for inmates to tattoo themselves, Kirk wanted the tattoos removed. Arrangements were made with a cosmetic surgeon to perform the operation. A variety of negotiations took place before this operation could be performed. CASE was again soliciting medical assistance outside the confines of the NTS. Federal Bureau of Investigation and Federal Bureau of Prisons regulations required that records be kept up on all identifying marks or scars. Federal approval for removal of the tattoos was requested and eventually granted. Thereafter, Kirk was able to wear short-sleeved shirts without embarrassment.

"PEOPLE-IZING"

People are effective managers and dispensers of tangible reinforcement, and they can also provide reinforcing social consequences for the behavior of others. People tend to associate with other people they enjoy. Such social interaction operates naturally, but it can be potentiated and heightened when it is programed. Frequently social interaction is used as a mediator between those who are working on a task and the impersonal task itself.

A program of "humanizing" or "people-izing" was developed through the CASE staff. The program checker served as the interface between the student and his academic work. Although each program checker delivered the same academic service, the students selected their checkers on the basis of social reinforcement. "You did well, Jack." "You look great in your new shirt." "How's your mother doing?" Such comments by checkers became important factors in their selection.

CASE staff were selected for their special abilities—their skill at "doing their own thing." The CASE storekeeper, who later became the cafeteria cook—although he was male and Irish—presented the warmth and responsiveness that are generally associated with the "Jewish mama" phenomenon. He was an affable and demonstrative "taking care of" person (each society should have at least one). The young law student appointed as librarian was black and politically active. He was sensitive to the needs of both black and white students. He became a model for the black students as well as an emotional trainer for the white southern students who entered CASE without any intimate knowledge of the intellectual range of black people and flaunted their bigotry.

The black and white female staff contributed to the socialization of the students. CASE students readily admitted that they dressed to please female staff as well as their families and guests. The students looked forward to lunch time and occasional discussions with staff about their problems with girl friends, mothers, or other members of the family. CASE II was designed to utilize the reinforcing properties of real life situations. This fostered community-oriented behavior. A community that cared and made demands, a community that permitted the student to investigate the range of his own potential, required the student to discriminate among the range of activities possible. He was led to select activities

103

that eventually paid off. These activities appeared to be critical in the development and maintenance of appropriate social behaviors.

The people-izing process also helped the students to survive the holiday season. Christmas in prison is usually a period of extreme depression. Youngsters away from home, any kind of home, experience a distinct loneliness at this holiday season. Although the CASE staff could not assume the role of family, its familial qualities helped sustain the youngsters during the holidays and on birthdays when parents or other members of the students' natural families did not visit or send even token gifts.

Unwanted effects can arise when staff is permitted to engage in intimate social relations with students. Too much closeness is potentially damaging to a demonstration program, for one of the critical functions of an operational research program is to design a system which can be maintained with staff members other than those originally selected. Frequently a demonstration plan is carried out successfully by one staff but fails completely when attempted by another. To determine the instructional and correctional needs of staffing similar operational research programs, the CASE administration conducted an experiment. All major teaching and correction staff were changed during the project term to ascertain whether CASE procedures would be maintained by a staff less wholeheartedly dedicated to the program than the original group. This, of course, created administrative problems. A number of direct confrontations resulted when new, untrained staff members were required to participate in CASE procedures that were alien to those practiced at the NTS. Problems arose from both individual and group resistance by these new staff members to the CASE program.

One of the new correctional staff was assigned as correctional supervisor for CASE and was charged with supervision of five other full-time or part-time officers. When that supervisor joined the program, he readily admitted that he felt the CASE project was unworkable and that he would never work out. He began his stay in CASE by attempting to manipulate the behavior of physically small and immature white students. He cultivated this group of favorite students and gathered them together each night for lengthy confidential discussions. These events were observed through the normal CASE procedure of recording all behaviors that led to bonuses and fines. It soon became clear that this officer was favoring a select group of students while alternately punishing or avoiding contact with others. In particular, he gave large bonuses to this group of young white males while recommending severe fines for large and physically mature black students. When the CASE administrator confronted this officer with the data which had been accumulated for more than a month, the officer did not deny the existence of preferential treatment for his favorites. He expressed his opinion "that not all students in CASE deserved to participate" in the behavior shaping and reinforcing system. He violently demanded that the project director either permit him to continue his method of student counseling and treatment or rotate him out of his position in the project. CASE immediately initiated a continuing in-service program for all new staff. This in-service training remained in force for the term of the project.

Within two months the NTS administration replaced this officer. Both the NTS and CASE staff admitted that such a program could not be easily conducted with staff who were openly opposed to the project. The remaining newly assigned officers continued their involvement in the project until its termination. Eventually, each demonstrated both a willingness and an ability to operate within the CASE program structure without negating their personal and idiosyncratic means of dealing with students. One result of the ability of CASE to maintain its operation productively despite prejudiced and contrarily-directed correctional staff was that *the administration of the NTS and the Federal Bureau of Prisons came to recognize the strength of CASE's specified procedures, rules, and regulations.*

SOCIALIZATION

Because CASE students were able to read, had well-lighted places to sit, were governed by rules which permitted reading under a variety of conditions, and experienced positive consequences for reading, they read a great deal. Lights remained on in private sleeping rooms long after midnight because some students became engrossed in their books. The traditional custodial policy of lights out at 9:00 or 10:00 o'clock in the evening is clearly detrimental to the development of persistent study and reading behaviors. Further, establishing an arbitrary policy of having a set day or hour when certain groups of students can visit the library to check out books also is detrimental to the development of persistent study and reading behaviors.

Because he had purchasing power, the CASE student was able to redesign his private room. This option tended to compete directly with the traditional ways that inmates spend leisure time in the evening (shooting pool, watching television, or jiving). In the latter half of the project, the amount of time CASE students spent in quiet discussions, reading, and study behaviors within the private rooms was greater than the time spent in the lounge, except during the weekends. Concurrently, the students learned to schedule their weekday evening hours in school work and letter writing, and they used the weekend hours for relaxation and outdoor activity. In general, the CASE students handled themselves like gentlemen throughout the program. The kinds and magnitude of violence and vulgarity that were exhibited in the traditional NTS programs were seldom demonstrated in CASE. The students were courteous to women, civil with each other, and enjoyed the mutual confidence that comes from living in an orderly and democratic society. This does not mean that the students never used traditional Anglo-Saxon words; far from it. They did learn what behaviors were appropriate in the various academic and social situations in CASE. For example, the use of vulgar language among themselves in their private rooms was all right, whereas such behavior simply did not occur in the presence of women at the dining table.

To be considered civilized, a human being must display a variety of social behaviors acceptable to the majority in his community. He must discriminate among various situations that require different responses, presenting the variety of verbal and behavioral skills that will be both reinforcing to and reinforced by others in his community. Such behavioral civility is a diplomatic art, and, in a sense, diplomacy is what the CASE community was shaping and reinforcing—the ability to deal with a range of people in a mutually acceptable way. Socialization of the CASE students was carried out by designing laws and procedures, providing models and learning programs, and applying appropriate consequences. Although money, goods, and services were reinforcing, there could be no doubt that one of the more powerful reinforcers used by the project in developing social skills was the people-izing influence of people.

Chapter 6 🙂🙂🙂🙂🙂🙂🙂🙂🙂🙂

Academic Results

🙂🙂🙂🙂🙂🙂🙂🙂🙂

*E*xplicit records of time, points, and correct responses on programs and tests were critical in determining the effect of various elements of the program. Changes in the program were instituted after baseline data had been established. To eliminate the effect of the general behavioral increase that accompanies the initiation of any new educational program, the initial six week period of data collection was considered part of the baseline operation. Along with the academic data collected during the educational workday, all other supporting events (spending patterns, use of leisure time, and so forth) were recorded and analyzed.

DATA GATHERING PROCEDURES

The staff of CASE was committed to analyzing the behavior of the individual student. Critical incidents were recorded in the behavioral notes and reviewed daily by the research staff. Neither a momentary fist fight in the lounge nor a student sleeping over his reading program went unreported. Throughout the project, up-to-date information concerning the earnings, spending, educational activities and performance, and social interactions of each student was readily available to assist the staff in making recommendations for academic and interpersonal programs. The individual student was clocked in and out of each area—the home floor, the educational area or test room, the cafeteria, the lounge, the infirmary, and the staff offices. This procedure provided an exact record for each individual, over hundreds of calendar days, in terms of activities in functional locations and time measured in hundredths of an hour. Transactions involving points earned and spent were carefully recorded to the penny. These procedures made possible the ongoing behavioral analysis of each student. Charts on which the information was recorded provided the data for later comparisons of variables of interest on a cross-sectional basis. Thus it was possible, for example, to assess students grouped according to categories such as "those 16 students present in CASE II for 272 or more days."

The behavioral objectives of the educational programing were expressed in the CASE II progress report, "Contingencies Applicable to Special Education of Delinquents: Establishing Twenty-Four Hour Control in an Experimental Cottage," which was submitted to the Office of Juvenile Delinquency and Youth Development on June 30, 1966 (Section III, page 11):

Five subject-matter areas have been identified as working divisions for curriculum development: (1) reading, (2) language usage, (3) mathematics, (4) science, and (5) social studies. Within each of these subject-matter areas, programs have been introduced in such a way that an entering student may: take diagnostic tests on the basis of which he may begin program work with the precise programs in which he has not yet scored 90 per cent accuracy; continue to work on programs in sequence so as to advance through a series of successes in small steps; go from any point of grade-level achievement to an open-ended level of higher achievement (grades one through twelve, and even beyond). This procedure tends to overcome the deficiencies of rigid grade-level placement for the individual student whose grade-level progress very often ranges from

109

one to five years from one subject to another. If a student is doing fourth-grade work in language usage and eighth-grade work in mathematics, for example, he may begin work in each of these areas at the stepping-point most appropriate to his present repertoire.

These behavioral objectives can be stated in more theoretical terms to clarify the meaning of open-ended progress. Many research studies have demonstrated the disastrous effects of teacher expectations which restrict artificially the potential performance of the student. Limited expectations can lead to programs designed to limit performance. The CASE staff assumed no ceiling to the human capacity for learning, either in the development of tool skills or in the mastery of topical content. If X is defined as a measurable unit of monthly progress feasible for a given individual student with unknown maximum and minimum range for probable occurrence unique to him alone within a given time, the objective of CASE II was to enable this student to advance at a rate approximating X-max grade levels per month, or twelve X-max grade levels per year as measured by the Stanford Achievement Test median grade level scores.

For each of the five curriculum areas, the objective was to enable the student to advance at a mean rate of X-max grade levels per month as measured by the corresponding subtests of the SAT battery. Within each of the curriculum areas—any one of which the student could choose to work on or not to work on at any time— the objective was to enable the student to perform at an accuracy rate of 90 per cent or better on specific programs, as measured by unit (lesson) criteria frames checked on unit completion and by both unit tests and final tests. In the specification of these criteria, it was recognized that the SAT had limitations of reliability and validity for this population. A number of variables were kept project-constant. The CASE administration resisted any changes which would have departed from the use of programed instruction as the primary learning medium, from basic procedures making points contingent upon behavior, or from the basic evaluative criteria.

Academic Results

The formal CASE II year was comprised of six major segments (see Figure 6). The first segment, the Project Orientation Period, was not used for detailed data analysis. The next four were specifically used for comparative educational data gathering. Each was characterized by a procedural and methodological approach somewhat different from the others (see Table 4). What remained constant was the use of programed instruction as an important feature of the educational method throughout the entire eight months. The program functions that varied were (1) the schedule of point reinforcement or payoff—there was a change toward payment only for measured achievement; (2) the number and variety of subject-matter programs available to the student—the curriculum grew and then stabilized; (3) the systematic use of organized classes

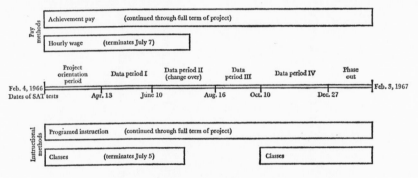

FIGURE 6.　CASE II Project Data Schedule

offered to the student for voluntary optional participation to supplement his programed instruction—an approach introduced experimentally to test its effectiveness only during the last two months under study. Each of these data periods was preceded and followed by issuance of national standardized tests and by pre- and post-program instruction tests.

During Period I (April 13 to June 10) planning and preparation continued. A basic curriculum of programed materials was developed and there were no systematic class offerings. The students were paid both by the hour and by their demonstrated

111

Table 4. MAIN VARIABLES IN EDUCATIONAL METHODOLOGY

Major Variables	*Period I*	*Period II*	*Period III*	*Period IV*
System of point reinforcement	Points for hourly wage and demonstrated achievement	Points for demonstrated achievement	Points for demonstrated achievement	Points for demonstrated achievement including class performance
Status of programed instruction curriculum	Increasing resources	Increasing resources	Stable	Stable
Supporting instruction	Individual help and seminars	Individual help and seminars	Individual help	Classroom courses and individual help

achievement in instructional programs. The hourly pay rate for educational activities varied according to the four grade levels of achievement: for freshmen (grades 1, 2, 3, 4)—twenty points per hour; for sophomores (grades 5, 6, 7)—thirty points per hour; for juniors (grades 8, 9, 10A)—forty points per hour; and for seniors (grades 10B, 11, 12)—fifty points per hour. The achievement required for promotion, and the prestige that went with promotion, were entirely objective (completion of designated programs) and were declared to the student by means of a sign plainly posted in the educational area.

With each promotion to a higher level the student earned an increment of ten points per hour. Pay for achievement in completing program units and tests was based on the previous experience of effective rates determined during CASE I. While this hourly-plus-achievement pay mode of reinforcement was in use, a basic curriculum was being established for reading, English, mathematics, science, and social studies. This curriculum was designed so that the student could proceed from any diagnosed grade level of achievement through the high school diploma if he was given enough time, an appropriate reinforcement, and timely teacher assistance.

During this period the teachers held seminars with the students but held only one formal daytime class. Effective telephone communication was presented for two weeks in May with daily one-hour sessions. Two evening classes—typing and electricity—were offered, but only a few students participated. These classes were not considered part of the regular CASE II curriculum.

Period II (June 11 to August 15) contained pilot tryouts of materials and procedures. On July 8, the hourly wage for educational work was dropped. The students had been told of this impending change months earlier. Point payoff thereafter was limited to measured progress in programs. Some curriculum additions took place. An effort was made to fill the gaps between programs, so that the newly added programs could help reduce the amount of teacher assistance needed for individual students. Some enrichment programs were also added, both to increase the options and to afford a medium for testing new programs for possible inclusion in the basic curriculum. One classroom course, Basic Teachings of Religion, was offered by the NTS Protestant chaplain from 2:00 to 3:00 P.M. on Tuesdays for the twelve weeks between June 14 and August 30. In essence, Period II was characterized by (1) a change to piecework pay for educational performance, (2) further refinement of the curricula, and (3) emphasis on programed instruction and deemphasis of classes. At the end of Period II, educational staff changes were made, facilitating more effective use of trained paraprofessionals (educational technologists) so that the professional teachers could concentrate upon the management of learning.

Period III (August 16 to October 10) was the test period of the stable programed instruction curriculum. The system of point reinforcement only for program progress was continued. Except for one final class and a post-testing session of the Basic Teachings of Religion class started early in Period II, no classroom courses were offered.

Period IV (October 11 to December 27) employed one methodological change: classroom courses were designed to supplement the programed instruction curricula. Point reinforcement was given for performance and progress in both classroom work and programed instruction. The programed curricula remained stable. All eight classes offered extended beyond the criterion test date (December 27) to within a week or so of the close of the data year in early February 1967.

The four time periods between testings were roughly comparable in the number of days that the students were involved in active learning efforts. Period II was not included in the more detailed analysis of student educational earnings, hours of study, and grade level gain, because resources for processing of data were limited. Instead, the data on only three periods are represented. The data on student progress in Period II were readily available and were easy to include in the analysis of variance technique. Data relevant to the student population during the CASE Interim period are also provided. In addition, data concerning students who trans-

Academic Results

ferred to NTS programs are included to assist in describing the termination of CASE II project operation.

Students were admitted to CASE singly or in groups of up to four students in any given ten day period (with one exception). The project reached its full complement of twenty-eight students in April 1966; as some of these students were paroled, other students were admitted. Seventeen students were originally admitted to CASE in February 1966. Four more were admitted in March, ten in April, two in both June and July, and three in both August and October. Students terminated their residency in Jefferson Hall singly or in groups of up to four students in any one month prior to the time all were transferred to the NTS in March 1967. At the closing date on February 3, twenty-two students were still assigned to CASE; the other nineteen had left prior to the data analysis closing date.

The forty-one students were present for a mean of 220.4 days of the data year. Five students were present for less than one-quarter of a year. Twelve were present for more than a quarter but less than half of a year. Nine were present for between one-half and three-quarters of a year. The remaining seventeen were CASE students for more than three-quarters of a year. Only thirty-six of the forty-one students who participated in CASE were taken into account for a presentation of general student progress in the curriculum. These were the thirty-six students who were present in the project for ninety or more days. The brief participation of the five students present for fewer than ninety days was due to two reasons: three students were holdover veterans from CASE I, and two escaped after less than two months with the project.

The proportion of students achieving at the lower half of the traditional twelve grades of school at the time of entry can be seen in Table 5, as can the proportion achieving successfully with curricular materials suited to the upper half of the twelve traditional grades at the time of departure. In English, 100 per cent of the students were functioning approximately within the range of the

115

Table 5. Student Placement in Curriculum Areas

CURRICULUM LEVEL

Curriculum Area	Entrance Placement								Terminal Achievement							
	Freshmen		Sophomores		Juniors		Seniors		Freshmen		Sophomores		Juniors		Seniors	
	#	%	#	%	#	%	#	%	#	%	#	%	#	%	#	%
Reading	8	26	13	37	14	37	1	0	1	6	10	28	14	40	11	26
English	35	97	1	3	0	0	0	0	3	8	12	33	9	26	12	33
Science	8	18	28	82	0	0	0	0	5	9	10	29	16	44	5	18
Mathematics	26	75	10	25	0	0	0	0	5	17	3	8	19	50	9	25
Social studies	12	33	24	67	0	0	0	0	2	6	13	36	7	19	14	39

freshmen = grades 1–4
sophomores = grades 5–7
juniors = grades 8–10A
seniors = grades 10B–12

elementary school grades at the time of their entry. But 59 per cent of these students were functioning at an eighth to twelfth grade level at the time of their departure from the project.

The actual number of academic self-instructional programs completed by the CASE students during the full-project duration of CASE II is shown by curriculum area in Table 6. One-fourth of the total program completions were in reading. The remaining curriculum areas showed a relatively balanced distribution of program completions. The later development of the social studies curriculum resulted in a slightly lower frequency of program completions. Programs in most areas were used daily during the first quarter of the project year; no social studies programs were in circulation during that quarter because they were in the process of being acquired and adapted for use.

The highest number and percentage of program completions were at the sophomore level. The students of CASE II completed 578 programs: 45 per cent were within the sophomore level (grades 5, 6, 7). Sophomore and junior (grades 8, 9, 10A) completions combined account for 74 per cent of the programs completed. The distribution of 19 per cent of the program completions at the freshman level (grades 1, 2, 3, 4) is in contrast with the 7 per cent accounted for by the senior level (grades 10B, 11, 12).

When the program completions of the CASE II students are detailed according to curriculum area within achievement level, certain patterns of student program use are apparent. These students completed only seven science programs within the freshman level. They were concentrating on developing more basic skills in reading, English, and arithmetic at the freshman level. Social studies rather than science emerged as the freshman curriculum area within which reading skills were most frequently used. More sophomore programs were completed in mathematics (176) than in science (134) and English (104). At the junior level, reading (139) and science (110) were most prominent, and mathematics (29) was as low as social studies (29) in frequency of completions. Students working at the senior level tended to record more completions in social studies (33) and reading (24) than in any of the other

Table 6. SELF-INSTRUCTIONAL PROGRAMS COMPLETED

	Freshman	Sophomore	Junior	Senior	Number Programs Completed in Subject	Total Programs Completed in Subject *Per Cent*
Reading	76	75	139	24	314	25
English	63	104	68	11	246	19
Mathematics	45	176	29	8	258	20
Science	7	134	110	8	259	20
Social studies	55	89	29	33	206	16
Number of Programs Completed in Grade Level	246	578	375	84	Total 1283	
Percentage of Total Completed in Grade Level	19	45	29	7		Total 100

three areas. The distribution of curriculum completions therefore emerges as one of the indicators of educational performance of the CASE II students.

The number of programs completed by students also reflects two other project variables: number of active study hours, and points earned for educational programs. Mean weekly student study hours for the three distinct data-gathering periods (I, III, and IV) in the project were computed. This analysis shows that mean student study hours during Period IV were significantly greater than during either Periods I or III. This could have been the result of the changes in any one or all three of the techniques employed. Student study hours during Periods I and III were compared to determine the effect of the two payment systems (see Figure 7). During Period I, students were paid for hours spent studying and for correct answers on programs and tests. During Period III, students were paid only for correct answers on programs and tests, but their total earnings were comparable to their earnings during Period I. This change in payment procedure appears to have been a major influence on the number of hours that students actually studied each day.

Two six-week series of data have been reduced to show the change in student study hours. One series occurred during Period I, immediately after the increase in available study hours but after two months of 28.75-hour weeks; the second series occurred during Period III, three months after the increase in available study hours. By precluding the effect of learning method variables, these two data series accurately reflect the impact of the increase in available study hours and the change in pay method on actual daily hours of study.

During Period I, the mean number of hours spent in study during each week day was erratic, with a dramatic increase in measured study activity on Thursday, the day before payday. The individual data reduced for this presentation show a wide range around the mean for Period I, but a much reduced range for Period III. In general, it may be said that during Period III a more consistent work pattern was evident than during Period I. The small

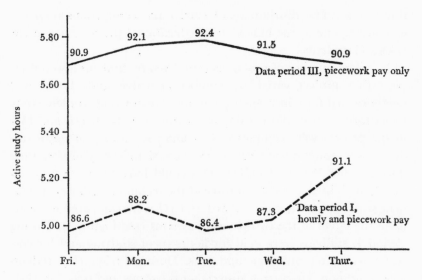

FIGURE 7. Mean Hours of Active Study Per Day

numerals above the graphic intersection points in Figure 7 refer to the mean percentage of time spent in study during the total study time available. During Period I, a grand mean of 87.9 per cent of available time was spent in study, or 5.06 mean hours per day. During Period III, students spent 91.6 per cent of the available time in active study, or 5.72 mean hours per day. This was an increase of .66 mean hours per day in study (or 40 minutes) after an increase of 30 available minutes per day. The students appear to have worked both actually and proportionally longer and more consistently during Period III than under the hourly pay system during Period I.

This change of work patterns influenced other project operations. One of the most dramatic results was the required rescheduling of teaching assistants from Thursdays (when the rush for program completions and checking was greatest) to more general (but as active) coverage for the entire week. A record of the points that students earned for academic study was available, in weekly totals, for the entire project. As for study hours, daily accounting

120

of this point earnings data was available for only three project data periods. The mean weekly point earnings for all students during the entire length of the project are presented in Figure 8. Unlike hours studied, point earnings over time show more of a relationship with a number of other project variables. Although these relationships are marked, some of them may be only coincidental (that is, no functional relation has been established through control procedures) or the result of seasonal (weekly, monthly, yearly) cyclic variation. They are reported here principally to indicate the longitudinal record of payment for educational activities.

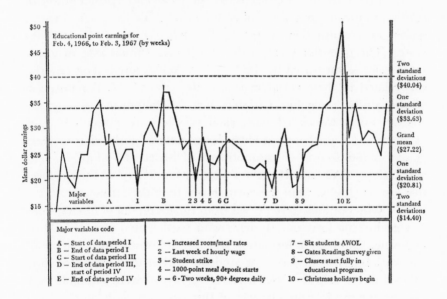

FIGURE 8.   Educational Program Point Earnings and Other Project Variables

One consistent pattern of earnings within each data period is evident: high earnings at the beginning, low earnings in the middle, and high earnings at the end. The principal cause for this was the administration of SAT tests (with high point payoff) at the beginning and ending of each period. Interperiod variation was

121

often associated with specifiable project variables other than student study activity. The variation in point earnings did, however, approximate a normal distribution. The only mean weekly point payments which fell beyond two standard deviations were at the start of the project and during December when high point payoff in classes (as incentive for maximum achievement and in preparation for purchasing Christmas gifts) coincided with the administration of SAT tests.

STANFORD ACHIEVEMENT TEST

Five variables were selected for particular consideration in relation to mean annual rate of gain on the SAT: race, age at entry, source of commitment, entry SAT grade scores, and entry IQ scores. The question was whether the mean annual rate of grade score gain, as measured by the Stanford Achievement Test criteria, was related to these variables in any important way. For purposes of this study, these five variables were dichotomized, and grade change scores associated with each subclass are presented: race (Caucasian/Negro), age at entry (over sixteen/under sixteen years of age), and source of commitment (District of Columbia/Federal). Entry SAT and IQ scores were dichotomized at their respective means (higher than the mean/lower than the mean).

Observations were drawn from the total pool of observations concerning the forty-one students who participated in CASE II at any time. Complete information was not uniformly available on all five variables for all forty-one students within the context of time limits and the criterion tests used. Observations were available concerning the grade score changes of thirty-two students on the 1953 series forms of the SAT. The time period delimited by the criterion tests of this series extended from December 1965 to December 1966. Observations were available concerning the grade score changes of thirty-one students on the 1963 series SAT. These students were not necessarily the same persons as those who had provided data concerning the 1953 series. The 1963 forms providing data on thirty-one students were administered between March 1966 and March 1967.

Table 7 shows the mean yearly rate of gain in the tests of the 1953 series across the five selected variables. The rate of gain in grade levels per year for all thirty-two students observed was 2.0 (this rate of gain is predicated on a twelve-month year of educational effort, rather than a nine-month or ten-month base). The 1953 norms were particularly appropriate to the instructional objectives evidenced in the programed materials used in CASE. Standards exemplified by the 1953 series of the SAT were apparently influential in the specification of instructional objectives for programed instruction developed between 1953 and 1963.

Differential results for the five variables indicated that prior educational achievement as measured by standardized tests discriminated most strongly as to rate of educational gain in the CASE II system. The thirty-two students were dichotomized according to their scores on the SAT at the time of entry. Students with high SAT scores at entry had a mean rate of gain of 2.6 grade levels per year, in contrast with a rate of 1.3 grade levels per year for students with a low SAT score at entry. *Race, IQ, and source of commitment were equal to each other under the criterion of mean rate of yearly gain on the 1953 series of the SAT.* The white student, the Federal student, or the student with the high IQ had a rate of gain of 2.2 grade levels per year, while the Negro student, the District of Columbia student, and the student with a low IQ level each had a rate of gain of 1.7 grade levels per year. The least differential among the five variables was observed for the age variable. The ten younger students, those under sixteen years of age at entry, had a rate of gain of 2.1 grade levels per year, as opposed to the rate of 1.9 grade levels per year for the twenty-two students over sixteen years of age at entry.

Table 8 shows the mean yearly rate of gain for the 1963 tests according to each of the five variables. The rate of gain for all thirty-one students was 1.5 grade levels per year. This was a half a grade level per year less than the rate of gain recorded for thirty-two students on tests of the 1953 series. The interpretation was made that the procedures were the same for the student, whether he was being assessed by the 1953 or 1963 SAT criteria of gain in

123

Table 7. GRADE SCORE CHANGES ON 1953 SERIES SAT, DECEMBER 1965 TO DECEMBER 1966

	Number of Students	Mean Number of Days Present	Actual Mean Grade Score Gain per Mean Days Present	Anticipated Mean Grade Score Rate of Gain for 365 Days
All students	32	227.13	1.22	2.0
Caucasian	16	221.69	1.36	2.2
Negro	16	232.56	1.09	1.7
Over 16 years at entry	22	215.64	1.10	1.9
Under 16 years at entry	10	252.40	1.49	2.1
Federal commitment	17	223.82	1.35	2.2
D. C. commitment	15	230.87	1.07	1.7
High SAT at entry	16	226.63	1.64	2.6
Low SAT at entry	16	227.63	0.81	1.3
High IQ Score at entry	16	238.56	1.44	2.2
Low IQ Score at entry	16	215.69	1.01	1.7

124

Table 8. GRADE SCORE CHANGES ON THE 1963 SERIES SAT, MARCH 1966 TO MARCH 1967

	Number of Students	Mean Number of Days Present	Actual Mean Grade Score Gain per Mean Days Present	Anticipated Mean Grade Score Rate of Gain for 365 Days
All students	31	226.61	.93	1.5
Caucasian	16	205.94	.78	1.4
Negro	15	248.67	1.10	1.6
Over 16 years at entry	22	207.82	.92	1.6
Under 16 years at entry	9	272.56	.97	1.3
Federal commitment	17	202.65	.68	1.2
D. C. commitment	14	255.71	1.23	1.8
High SAT at entry	17	212.41	.72	1.2
Low SAT at entry	14	243.86	1.19	1.8
High IQ at entry	18	206.06	.61	1.1
Low IQ at entry	13	270.92	1.38	1.9

125

educational achievement. The student rose to whatever standards were set by the programed instructional objectives. It so happened that the objectives of the programed materials used by CASE were more in keeping with the 1953 norms. This finding was judged to have important implications for instructional programing in interaction with educational procedures. The conclusion can be drawn that programed materials should be revised more frequently than they actually are in order to keep up with changing norms.

Differential results under the 1963 SAT criteria were in dramatic contrast with results for the 1953 series. The student with a low IQ at entry (as determined by ranking within the full complement of forty-one students) had a rate of gain of 1.9 grade levels per year on the 1963 norms, as opposed to a rate of 1.1 grade levels per year for the student with a high IQ. Students with low entry SAT scores did better than those with high SAT scores at entry: 1.8 as opposed to 1.2 grade levels per year. The same contrast prevailed for District of Columbia students over students present under Federal commitment. The older students and the Negro students were groups whose mean rate of gain was 1.6 grade levels per year, as opposed to a correspondingly lower rate of annual gain for the white students and the younger students. Under this criterion, therefore, the results were diametrically opposed to the results of the 1953 series testing. One explanation for this discrepancy was that the 1963 tests tended to be administered to the students who were in the project longest or latest. The first test of the 1963 series was administered in March 1966 and the last in March 1967. The 1953 series tests were used from December 1965 through December 1966. A check of the mean number of days present for students taking tests of the two series revealed that there was little difference in length of stay with the project; rounding of the resultant mean indicated that it was 227 days for each group. A more important difference may well have been the delimitation of each time period within the total fifteen-month span (from the first 1953 series test in December 1965 to the last 1963 series test in March 1967).

It is possible that increasingly more rigorous standards were interacting with the increasing stabilization of the project. The project may have been getting set in its procedural ways and getting rid of its initial stimulus change (Hawthorne effect). Presumably the project would have increased rather than decreased its efficacy if it had functioned longer. This point of view is predicated on the opportunity to set increasingly higher standards in the educational program as time went on. The initial assumption made by the CASE II investigators was that they acknowledged no ceiling to the capacity for student educational achievement. At the conclusion of the project, the investigators still knew no ceiling for this capacity but recognized that the capacity was higher than the goals that had been established for operational purposes.

The mean educational hours, earnings, and the mean grade score changes on the five SAT subtests for Periods I, III, and IV are presented with their standard deviations in Table 9.

Table 9. MEANS AND STANDARD DEVIATIONS FOR EDUCATIONAL HOURS, POINT EARNINGS, AND GRADE SCORE CHANGE

Variable Number and Name	Mean	S.D.
1 Educational hours, Period I	147.56 hours	39.13
2 Educational hours, Period III	129.86 hours	41.08
3 Educational hours, Period IV	173.70 hours	59.89
4 Point earnings, Period I	133.89 dollars	61.43
5 Point earnings, Period III	153.81 dollars	73.23
6 Point earnings, Period IV	247.36 dollars	104.24
ª7 Grade score change, Period I	+.21 grade	0.48
ª8 Grade score change, Period III	+.37 grade	0.64
ª9 Grade score change, Period IV	+.63 grade	0.73

ª Each one-month period should show an average increase of .08 for public school students.

In the original plan, these time periods were to have been of approximately equal duration. Exigencies of administration, however, made one of the data periods, Period IV, notably longer than the others. Direct comparisons among the means could not therefore be made. Period IV had approximately 1.34 times as many days of educational activities as did Periods I and III. A quality control approach was attempted, but the hazards of estimation precluded much of the value that this method was originally hoped to have.

Analysis of variance techniques was used to analyze the grade changes in SAT scores for sixteen students within four time periods of approximately two months each. Each of these periods was characterized by a different procedural or methodological approach to implementing a programed instruction curriculum. Seven subtests of the Stanford Achievement Test battery were analyzed separately.

Statistically significant differences were found to be associated with treatment periods for paragraph meaning, language usage, and social studies. The greatest gains in paragraph meaning were recorded for Period IV, the period characterized by achievement pay, a stable curriculum, and classroom courses supplementing programed instruction. Although high gains marked Period IV for language usage as well, this was interpreted as the result of using a changed form of the SAT as a criterion from one testing to the next. The notably poor performance of the low payoff students for language usage during Period II was also understood to have been the result of this criterion problem. In social studies, Period III was found to be the period of outstanding progress, and the hypothesis that achievement incentives without supplementary classes was a more effective approach for the teaching of social studies could not be rejected. The students with high earnings showed a statistically significant superiority of performance as measured by grade level gain in arithmetic reasoning.

The average monthly rate of grade level gain for these students in each curriculum area is presented in Table 10. The average expected increase in the United States public schools is .08 levels per month.

Reading, English, mathematical reasoning, and science were thus seen to be areas in which the CASE II students demonstrated important skill development through programed instruction. Arithmetic computation and social studies were noted to be skill areas

Academic Results

Table 10. Monthly Grade Level Gain

Curriculum Area	Level
Paragraph meaning	.17
Language usage	.28
Spelling	.20
Arithmetic reasoning	.16
Arithmetic computation	.10
Science	.16
Social Studies	.11

which would have to receive lower efficiency ratings. The evidence suggested that the use of achievement incentives without supplementary classes is one means to improve efficiency for social studies. Supplementary classes did not prove more effective for the establishment and maintenance of behaviors demonstrating the mastery of social studies information.

Language usage was the skill most effectively promoted. This result was not in any way compromised by criterion ambiguity, since the first and final tests in the series were of the same series of forms. The grade score changes were, in fact, deflated values, adjusted to bring them into closer conformity to the norms of the 1963 series and therefore more on a par with contemporary standards.

Two factors emerged as especially important in the operation of a programed instructional system. One was that scheduling of the reinforcements deserves thorough planning in the total program design. The other was staff attention as a reinforcer.

ARMY REVISED BETA

Whether increased scores on IQ tests reflect a true change in basic intelligence or simply an enhanced level of acculturation, less test anxiety, or the acquisition of test-taking skills, the fact remains that of the twenty-four students tested at entry to the NTS and retested in the CASE project, twenty-three demonstrated an increase in IQ scores and only one remained the same.

Scores for IQ at entry were available for forty of the full complement of forty-one students who participated in the project's activities at any time during the period between February 4, 1966, and February 3, 1967. No IQ score was available for one student who escaped very shortly after his arrival. For these forty students, the mean of the IQ scores on the Revised Beta was 93.5 with a standard deviation of 9.98. The lowest IQ score of any of the forty students was 67. The highest was 112. With an interval of 10 IQ points specifying a frequency class, it was found that the modal class for IQ scores at admission was the 90.0 to 99.9 range. Seventeen students had IQs recorded within these limits.

On December 20, 1966, twenty-four students were retested on the Revised Beta. This was the total number of students present for testing at that time and did not constitute a selected group. The frequency distribution of IQ scores recorded for these twenty-four students at entry to the National Training School (see Figure 9) indicates that IQ scores from 90 to 99.9 were again the modal class. The class of next highest frequency was the 100 to 109.9 category. The general pattern was similar when the distribution of the twenty-four scores was compared with the distribution of the forty scores. However, at entrance a number of students who were not present for the second administration of the Revised Beta in December 1966 scored in the 90 to 109.9 range. This did not compromise the results of the later administration of the test but served as a frame of reference for the results which follow.

A comparison between the mean of the IQ scores at entry and the mean of the IQ scores for the same twenty-four students on December 20, 1966, shows their mean gain was 12.5 IQ points. These results represented statistically significant changes in their IQ scores at the .001 level. Only one student failed to show a gain. One student gained 27 IQ points. The range of the scores in the testing of December 20, 1966, extended from a low of 83 to a high of 121. The mean interval of time which had elapsed between testings was approximately seven months.

The pattern of change in frequency distribution of IQ scores for these students from entry to December 1966 reveals the dramatic increase in scores. Sixteen of the twenty-four had scored below 100 at entry to NTS. In December, only six of the twenty-four scored below 100. In the December testing the IQ score modal class was between 110 and 119.9, an increase from the entrance testing in which the modal class had been between 90 and 99.9.

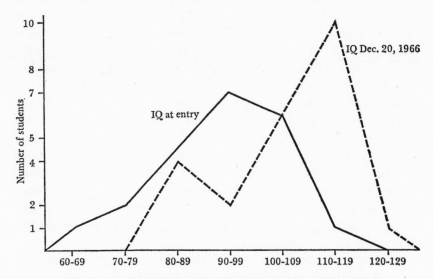

FIGURE 9.   Frequency Distribution of IQ Scores for
Twenty-Four Students

On March 20, 1967, nineteen of the twenty-four students were again tested. This group had a mean entry IQ of approximately 92.1, with a range from 67 to 112. The March mean score was approximately 108.3, and the range of scores extended from 77 to 126.

The results of the testing of March 1967 tended to confirm the reliability of the gains recorded in December 1966. The changes in both instances had high statistical significance, beyond the .01 level, and mere chance variation was therefore ruled out with a high degree of probability. The December testing showed an increase of 12.5 IQ points for twenty-four students. The March results showed

131

a mean increase of 16.2 IQ points for nineteen students from the time of their admissions testing.

Both the literature of clinical psychology and the personal experience of the psychologists associated with CASE II support the hypothesis that practice effect on the three test administrations of the revised Beta was negligible in increasing the scores. It was felt, however, that an analysis of individual students' results and of the differences within and between subtests should be undertaken. Subtests 2, 3, and 5 were considered to be those most readily influenced by memory and practice and were given particular attention. Results of the analysis indicated that neither these subtests nor any others could be said to account for as much as one half of the average gain in IQ score. It was also found that in no case could the increased score of any one student be attributed to better production in only one or two areas of mental functioning as measured by the Revised Beta. In the absence of evidence to the contrary, these IQ changes were taken to reflect across-the-board increases in the demonstration of ability. This applied to such areas of mental functioning as attention to detail, frustration tolerance, deductive reasoning, and acculturation.

Speculation as to why a steady increase in IQ scores was evidenced for these students brought out a number of possibilities. It was suggested that the students responded to the second and third administration of the test with greater enthusiasm and determination, since high scores were rewarded by a generous point payoff in proportion to the score; also, it was suggested that they were able to score higher because they had been exposed to a wider variety of intellectually stimulating material. The most important implication for the investigators was that a large group of people in our society fail to qualify for military service, further education and training, jobs, promotions, and so forth, not because of congenital disability but because of inadequate preparation and poor representation of chains of consequences. CASE II refined certain procedures which showed promise for overcoming these obstacles.

Chapter **7** ⟨≋≋≋≋≋≋≋≋≋≋≋≋≋≋≋⟩

What Happened to the Students?

⟨≋≋≋≋≋≋≋≋≋≋≋≋≋≋≋≋⟩

*T*he principal objective of CASE was the development of appropriate academic behavior. Social behavior within the project was shaped, maintained or modified insofar as it pertained to academic behaviors. No assumptions were made regarding the effect of the project on the student's adjustment when he returned to the community. Penal authorities and other interested professionals would gauge the value of this academically-based program as much by the rate of recidivism (reinstitutionalization) as by the increase of academic repertoires. To make an evaluation of recidivism possible, a grant to follow up these students was awarded to the Institute for Behavioral Research in July 1969.[1]

The following data indicate that CASE students stayed out of trouble longer than a similar group processed by the National Training School. During the first year the recidivist rate was two-thirds less than the norm. The data indicate that by the third year

[1] Center for the Study of Alternatives to Punishment in Maintaining Law and Order, National Institute of Law Enforcement and Criminal Justice, Law Enforcement Assistance Association #NI 047.

133

the total recidivist rate for CASE students may be near the norm. The CASE program evidently delayed the delinquent's return to incarceration, but his behavior would require additional maintenance in the real world for the CASE experience to remain effective after the first year in preventing recidivism.

During the winter of 1969, contact with the former CASE II students was made in several ways.[2] Information received aperiodically from the District of Columbia Jail, the Bureau of Prisons, and the Federal Bureau of Investigation showed that some former CASE students were in custody. These institutions were contacted. If the students were still in custody, permission was received and arrangements were made for interviews and testing. With one exception, all students confined in out-of-state institutions were interviewed by telephone. The Legal and Educational Alternatives to Punishment Project (LEAP) arranged for a member of each institution's teaching staff to administer the testing.

Former students confined in local (District of Columbia metropolitan area) institutions (and in one out-of-town state institution) were interviewed and tested by a LEAP staff member who traveled to those institutions. Students not in confinement were contacted either through their parole officers or by telephone calls or letters to their last known address. Local students and four from outside the District of Columbia area were brought into the Institute for Behavioral Research for their interviews and tests. The remaining out-of-town students were interviewed by telephone and tested by a LEAP staff member who traveled to their communities.

Information was gathered on thirty-one of the forty-one students. Of these thirty-one students, twenty-six were interviewed and tested; two were contacted and interviews and testing scheduled; and one, in the United States Army in Vietnam, was not contacted. Two other students had warrants pending for their arrest on viola-

[2] Excerpted and paraphrased from the Second Quarterly Report of the Legal and Educational Alternatives to Punishment Project (LEAP), the program which funded the CASE II follow-up.

tions of parole and could not be located. Of the ten students about whom no information could be obtained, seven had commitments from the District of Columbia, and three had been Federal commitments from Alabama, California, and Michigan.

Some difficult questions must be answered before evaluating the data. For example, is a student to be considered a CASE student if he was in the program for only four months, ran away, and was incarcerated for over two years at another penal institution? What about students who were in CASE five months and then stayed at the National Training School for an additional fourteen months before release? Preliminary discussions with others in the field of juvenile delinquency suggested that students not released directly from the program, or not released within ninety days after leaving CASE, should not be considered in the CASE data because their involvement with other programs would confound the data.

Four of the thirty-one students were not included in this review because they were in the CASE program less than ninety days (fifteen to seventy-four days). Of the remaining twenty-seven students, eleven were released directly from CASE, and sixteen moved from CASE to other programs or institutions before final release. Of the eleven students released directly from CASE, three recidivated in the first year (27.3 per cent), none between thirteen and twenty-four months, and one after twenty-five to thirty-six months (9 per cent), making a total of four recidivists for a rate of 36.4 per cent. Of the remaining sixteen students released from other penal programs (between one month and two and a half years later), ten recidivated in the first year (62.5 per cent); one in the next twelve months (6.3 per cent); and none in the last year, making a total of eleven recidivists for a rate of 68.8 per cent (see Table 11). Although the numbers statistically are small, there appears to be a sharp difference in recidivism rate between those students released directly from the program and those who continued to serve terms elsewhere. Previous National Training School data indicate that 76 per cent of similar juveniles recidivate during the first year.

A preliminary review of the Gates Reading Survey and Stanford Achievement Test Battery scores indicates an unusual level of

Table 11. PRELIMINARY RECIDIVISM ANALYSIS

	Total in Category	0–12 Mos.	%	13–24 Mos.	%	25–36 Mos.	%	Over 36 Mos.	Total R	Total %
All students (released directly from CASE program)	11	R = 3	27.3	R = 0		R = 1	9.1	R = 0	R = 4	36.4
All students (from CASE to other programs or institutions before release)	16	R = 10	62.5	R = 1	6.3	R = 0		R = 0	R = 11	68.8
I. All Students	27	R = 13	48.1	R = 1	3.7	R = 1	3.7	R = 0	R = 15	55.6
D.C. students (released directly from CASE program)	3	R = 1	33.3	R = 0		R = 0		R = 0	R = 1	33.3
D.C. students (from CASE to other programs or institutions before release)	8	R = 4	50.0	R = 1	12.5	R = 0		R = 0	R = 5	62.5
II. D.C. Students	11	R = 5	45.4	R = 1	9.1	R = 0		R = 0	R = 6	54.5
Federal students (released directly from CASE program)	8	R = 2	25.0	R = 0		R = 1	12.5	R = 0	R = 3	37.5
Federal students (from CASE to other programs or institutions before release)	8	R = 6	75.0	R = 0		R = 0		R = 0	R = 6	75.0
III. Federal Students	16	R = 8	50.0	R = 0		R = 1	6.3	R = 0	R = 9	56.3

NOTE: Recidivists (R) are indicated by number of months since final date of incarceration.

Table 12. STANFORD ACHIEVEMENT TEST

	Word Mean.	Para. Mean.	Spell	Word/ Study	Lang. Usage	Comp.	Arithmetic Concept.	Arithmetic Appl.	Soc. St.	Sci.	Average
N+[a]	NA	3	7	NA	3	1	4	5	5	5	3
N[a]	NA	17	9	NA	12	13	10	6	8	7	16
N−[a]	NA	2	4	NA	6	8	5	5	3	4	3
Average of increase	NA	1.6	2.7	NA	2.1	1.6	2.5	2.6	2	2.6	1.7
Average of decrease	NA	−2.45	−2.25	NA	−1.95	−2.35	−1.76	−2.4	−2.1	−1.58	−1.4
Average of deviants[b]	NA	−0.02	+0.90	NA	−0.60	−1.91	+0.13	+0.28	+0.46	+0.74	+0.1

[a] N+ = number of students having a grade level increase of at least 1 year.

N = number of students having a grade level increase or decrease of less than 1 year.

N− = number of students having a grade level decrease of at least 1 year.

[b] Deviants means increase or decrease greater than 1 year.

retention in such subjects as spelling, math, and reading. In some cases reading scores were higher by over two years. Some of these students retained or increased their skills while they were out of school. Regular students in the Maryland counties of Montgomery and Prince Georges who have been tested by the Institute for Behavioral Research often show a drop of one to three years in their test grade scores after they have been out of school three months or more. IBR is searching for national test data on dropouts to help ascertain the differences in the academic retention rates of CASE students as compared to a national baseline. Retention data from similar juvenile populations—state or Federal—would be most useful. Listed below are academic retention data on the students tested thus far. Variations in the number of students indicated for the SAT subtests (see Table 12) are a result of either a change in the battery administered or an incomplete battery for one of the testings.

The data in Table 13 show the average grade level change and average of deviants for the Gates Reading Survey. The Gates

Table 13. GATES READING SURVEY

	Speed	Vocabulary	Compre- hension	Average
N+	14	9	10	11
N	9	13	12	13
N−	2	3	3	1
Average of increase	+2.7	+2	+2.3	+1.8
Average of decrease	−2.9	−2.2	−2.2	−1.8
Average of deviants	+2.0	+0.95	+1.26	+1.5

Reading Survey is included to help corroborate the reading score increase shown during CASE and to give some additional data on speed, vocabulary, and comprehension in reading. Since the majority of these students had not been in an academic setting for over two years when they were tested, this retention seems unusually good. National data is being sought on retention of academic information by high school graduates or dropouts.

THE CASE FOR CASE

The objective products of the CASE research were the students' tests, records, time spent, money earned, and the behaviors learned. The life dramas of these young men—the interpersonal and attitudinal changes in group social behaviors—are reflected in Army Revised Beta Intelligence tests. Transition from a harsh punitive prison treatment system to a positive reinforcing approach of "earn while you learn" created attitudinal changes in both staff and students. Although CASE did not set out to measure these behavioral changes objectively, the increase in wealth and know-how, which was measurable, permitted a subjective assessment of each student's new sense of worth. Purchasing power, an essential ingredient in any society, can be a powerful change agent. The CASE students were from poor and uneducated families. Poverty and ignorance produce a tight subculture within which the means to economic change are limited. Inability to purchase and lack of the educational skills necessary to participate in the mainstream of American life had forced these young people to "self-ghetto" themselves in small communities on the periphery of the larger society. The result was a group of adolescents who not only dropped out of school but in a real sense dropped out of life.

The project dealt with these dropouts from life. They were young men who had not succeeded in our society. They lived with frustration and anger, the results of failure. In fact, their schools had programed them for failure. The question we were asking was, "How could we program success for these youths in a penal environment which has historically been aversive and restrictive?" In the project the individual was not forced to do anything. This was against the basic CASE philosophy. If a student did not work or participate in the program, he received the same subsistence as the students in the rest of the National Training School. He could better

139

his lot by working hard, but he could not make it worse by not working. The rationale was that the young man had to recognize that he could better himself through his own efforts.

When the students first entered CASE, they asked a simple and basic question, "Man, what's in it for me?" The staff made sure they continued to ask that same question. The students were reminded, "If there is nothing in it for you, don't do it." And there was something in it for them. At the beginning it was points, money. Each student needed points to pay for his room, board, and clothing. He could choose to go on relief (to live as did the rest of the students at the National Training School), but that was not very reinforcing or dignified because all students in CASE had the opportunity to work and to earn more.

CASE students were paid for learning. A marginal wage-earner, behind in his study, could take one of the house jobs. However, he soon found out that he could make more money with more education. At CASE, study paid off more handsomely than sweeping floors. For example, one course program—English 2200—spanned eleven study units and thirteen tests. Successful completion of the series was worth 3,459 points—$34.59. A freshman working as a janitor three hours a night would take home only 1400 points in a week's time, a bare subsistence.

The project increased educational skills, particularly academic skills. Extrinsic reinforcements were used to initiate and motivate the students. After about four months, the students found that they could negotiate the CASE environment. They were able to divert a large amount of aggression to productive work, to learning. CASE was able to remove the officers during the weekly day shift. CASE helped all the students learn to read and write and to become involved in the academic system. CASE programed them for success.

The reader may wonder why CASE bothered. Why take youngsters who have experienced six to ten years of failure in a public school system and habilitate them? First, society's standard is that children from six to sixteen years of age will participate in education. The writers are not making moral judgments about why

140

we should or should not educate our youngsters. It is a societal decision that young men and women should go to school. For each youngster to feel that he is part of the mainstream of American life, he must perform successfully so that he can join the majority. Otherwise he is forced to join those who have not made it. Proof is available in the history of any CASE student.

The ability to purchase can lead to pride of ownership. This became obvious in the students' rented rooms. The amount of time and funds spent on the small enclosure the student called his private room indicated clearly that privacy and ownership were strong reinforcers. Comments indicated possessiveness: "Get out of my room; this is my room. I paid eight hundred points for this room; this is my room." For most students, this was the first time they could call a space their own and tell others to get out. As a result, the students tended to stay in their rooms more and more. The lounge became less appealing as the student rooms became places to have friends in, watch television, do homework, or write letters. The students started moving toward middle class adolescent life. They seemed to enjoy it, and they were willing to pay a high fee for that privilege.

When one young man came to CASE in the early part of the program, he said that there was something wrong with him. He felt that he was a misfit and could not do anything well except the antisocial behaviors. Even then he wasn't very bright—he got caught. In less than one year's time, this youth learned to succeed. And when he started to succeed in academic subject matter after eight years in public school, where he had considered himself incapable and stupid, his whole approach to education and to life changed. He became a man who enjoyed the sweet smell of success. An important fact of life that all people have come to recognize is that *success is one of the most powerful reinforcers for more activity, for more success*. The CASE project made it possible for this reinforcer to operate.

The basic premise CASE used with the students was that *the individual is always right*. He is right because his behavior is a response to the system. The thief is working for the reinforcer—the pay-off, the stolen goods. The careworn statement that crime doesn't pay does not hold up. Most of these youngsters had a higher rate of thefts than of convictions. One young man had stolen eighteen cars before he was caught. A successful car thief keeps stealing. This payoff and peer reinforcement seemed to maintain his behavior. If we change the cues and the system which maintained his performance (change the reinforcer and extinguish the antisocial behavior), we make it possible for the young man to change. The CASE project was a subculture, a miniature society designed and programed to effect this self-change.

In a traditional training school, or any other penal system where an individual is incarcerated, he is told what to do and how to do it. He lives by the aversive penal rules that have been established. He is told when to get up in the morning, when to go to eat, how to clean up, how to make his bed, where to walk, and how to march. He is never given an opportunity to make decisions on his own. The society says "do what we say or be punished" and is so programed that the establishment makes all the decisions for the youth. The CASE program did not follow the traditional penal premise, a premise that can prepare youth only for release into a fascist police state where everyone is told what to do and how to do it. The traditional penal system *does not prepare inmates for life in a democratic society.* (For a comparison of CASE II students and the regular NTS population, see Appendix A.)

In the CASE program, the individual made his own decisions: how he dressed, what he ate, when he went to bed, and how he spent his time and money. Whether he worked was his decision. These choices were essential. It was critical that the young man learn to make these decisions because in a democratic society he has to accept the consequences of his own decisions. Those programs—in public and private schools, penal or mental institutions—that do not give the youth an opportunity to make decisions and to fail or succeed in his decisions do not prepare him for coping with real-life problems. It is through this process of making decisions and experiencing consequences—failures and successes—that the individual can begin to evaluate his own performance.

Four years have passed since we closed the CASE II project

at Jefferson Hall. Since that closing, and because of the knowledge gained, we have brought contingency management and education technology into community public schools. As of 1971, we are serving over four hundred normal elementary school children and ninety special education students, and we have initiated special programs for one thousand pre-adjudicated delinquents. By 1972 we will have trained enough public school staff to develop and operate new academic and interpersonal programs in more than eighteen public schools in Maryland and Washington, D. C. The CASE II project has influenced the nation's juvenile corrections system. The new Kennedy Youth Center in West Virginia, which replaces the old National Training School in Washington, D. C., has maintained much of the CASE program.

It is the authors' conviction that the only effective approach to juvenile delinquency is the development of effective academic and interpersonal programs within our nation's public schools. We must stop building prisons for youth and begin investing our funds and energy to establish preventive systems within our present ongoing schools and community centers. The present interest by school boards in performance contracting, programed instruction and even student pay for summer school attendance indicates a strong trend toward setting behavioral objectives and finding contingencies to direct the student toward these academic goals. America is facing up to the problems created by a bankrupt educational and juvenile penal system. It has stopped attacking its youths as immoral, sick, and genetically incompenent and has come to recognize that a non-reinforcing environment, improperly maintained, does not produce academic and interpersonal competence.

Comparison of Case II and the National Training School for Boys

T he research nature of the CASE II project produced a vast amount of data available for comparison with the National Training School. However, data collected by NTS is limited to what is necessary for its daily operations. Therefore, comparability between the CASE II project and the NTS was determined by the amount and type of information collected by and available from both facilities for similar periods of time.

The NTS information concerning student population averages and staff assignments presented in this section was taken from the NTS Fact Sheet published on February 14, 1967. The information period covered by this fact sheet most nearly approximates the period of time that CASE II was in operation at that institution. Information concerning student population statistics is taken from Population Statistics Sheets of March 3, 1966, giving the population

Comparison of CASE II and NTS

statistics for January 1, 1966, and of February 14, 1967, giving the population statistics for January 1, 1967.

NTS information concerning specific educational achievement scores, such as scores for the Gates Reading Survey and the Stanford Achievement Test, were not available for a comparative period of time. Therefore, academic achievement comparison is limited to SAT scores at admission presented on the NTS Fact Sheet dated February 14, 1967.

To compare the forty-one CASE II students to the total NTS population it is necessary to present a profile of the NTS student population on January 1, 1966, and on January 1, 1967. This comparison is made for categories of data made available by the NTS: type of commitment (Table 14), type of offense (Table 15), religious background (Table 16), and cultural group (Table 17). The first date, January 1, 1966, was approximately one month before the start of the CASE II project at the NTS. The second, January 1, 1967, was approximately one month before the close of the project's full operation, the end of its data period. The second NTS student population profile is directly compared to the CASE II population on that same date, January 1, 1967. These three profiles are then compared to a profile of all forty-one CASE II students.

Of the seven CASE II students listed as "Other" in the presentation of all forty-one students in Table 15, one was committed for attempted housebreaking, one for violation of the Selective Service Act (printing registration cards), three for parole violation, and two for being beyond parental control.

It should be noted that the total of 244 students indicated for the NTS on January 1, 1966, is three more than the 241 students claimed as the population on that date. An attempt was made to determine the reason for these additional entries, which appear only in the "Type of Offense" category. In lieu of any satisfactory explanation the number of 244, as reported on the NTS Population Statistics Sheet, is given.

145

Table 14. COMPARISON OF COMMITMENTS

| | National Training School | | | | CASE II Project | | | |
| | Jan. 1, 1966 | | Jan. 1, 1967 | | Jan. 1, 1967 | | 41 Students | |
Type of Commitment	Number	Per Cent	Number	Per Cent	Number	Per Cent	Number	Per Cent
Federal Juvenile Delinquency Act	138	57.2	133	55.4	14	53.8	22	53.7
District of Columbia juveniles	98	40.7	99	41.2	12	46.2	19	46.3
Observation	5	2.1	3	1.2	0	0	0	0
Youth Corrections Act	0	0	5	2.2	0	0	0	0
Totals	241	100.0	240	100.0	26	100.0	41	100.0

Table 15. COMPARISON OF OFFENSES

| | National Training School | | | | CASE II Project | | | |
| | Jan. 1, 1966 | | Jan. 1, 1967 | | Jan. 1, 1967 | | 41 Students | |
Type of Offense	Number	Per Cent	Number	Per Cent	Number	Per Cent	Number	Per Cent
Dyer Act (auto theft)	136	55.7	126	52.5	12	46.2	18	43.9
Housebreaking	29	11.9	34	14.2	2	7.7	4	9.8
Postal violations	16	6.6	15	6.2	2	7.7	2	4.9
Petty larceny	14	5.7	7	3.0	2	7.7	3	7.3
Robbery	13	5.3	11	4.6	3	11.5	3	7.3
Assault	8	3.3	13	5.4	1	3.8	3	7.3
Homicide	3	1.2	1	0.4	1	3.8	1	2.4
Other	25	10.2	33	13.7	3	11.5	7	17.1
Totals	244	99.9	240	100.0	26	99.9	41	100.0

Table 16. Comparison of Religious Backgrounds

Religious Background	National Training School				CASE II Project			
	Jan. 1, 1966		Jan. 1, 1967		Jan. 1, 1967		41 Students	
	Number	Per Cent	Number	Per Cent	Number	Per Cent	Number	Per Cent
Catholic	67	27.8	70	29.2	7	26.9	9	21.9
Protestant	174	72.2	170	70.8	19	73.1	32	78.0
Totals	241	100.0	240	100.0	26	100.0	41	99.9

Table 17. Racial Comparison

Racial Comparison	National Training School				CASE II Project			
	Jan. 1, 1966		Jan. 1, 1967		Jan. 1, 1967		41 Students	
	Number	Per Cent	Number	Per Cent	Number	Per Cent	Number	Per Cent
Indian	6	2.5	6	2.5	0	0	0	0
Negro	113	46.9	126	52.5	13	50.0	20	48.8
White	122	50.6	108	45.0	13	50.0	21	51.2
Totals	241	100.0	240	100.0	26	100.0	41	100.0

A New Learning Environment

Table 18. COMPARISON OF STUDENT POPULATIONS AT ENTRY

Description at Entry	National Training School	All Students CASE II Project
Revised Beta	Low Average	91.1
SAT Score	7.7	5.7
Age	17	16.9

The figures on religious background, racial origin, and entry data clearly indicate the similarity between the CASE II and NTS populations. Racial balance was a primary target in the selection of students for CASE II. Just prior to the start of the project the majority of NTS students were white, but it was estimated that this would shift toward a 50 per cent balance of Negro and white students. Religious background was not given primary consideration in the selection process for assignment. Also, educational achievement was not a selection factor since both the Revised Beta and the Stanford Achievement Tests were issued after the students had been assigned to CASE. It is interesting to note (See Table 18) that on initial Stanford Achievement testing the CASE II students scored an average of two grades lower than did the NTS students. Both groups initially tested in the same range on the Revised Beta.

OPERATIONAL COMPARISONS

Staff: The equivalent of 18 full time and 4.8 part-time staff members were employed by the CASE II project. A total of forty-two different staff members were needed to fill these positions. This indicates some of the staffing difficulties which confronted the project. Of the forty-two employees, eighteen worked part-time schedules from one-quarter to three-quarter time. Employee stay with the project ranged from two weeks to the full project year. A comparison between the NTS and CASE II personnel is shown in Table 19.

Using figures on average daily student populations for both NTS and CASE II, a meaningful relationship can be shown. Table

148

Table 19. Comparison of Personnel

	FULL TIME				PART TIME			
	N.T.S.		CASE II[a]		N.T.S.		CASE II[a]	
Assignment	Number	Per Cent	Number	Per Cent	Number	Per Cent	Number	Per Cent
Research	0	0	4.0	22.2	0	0	0.3	6.3
Teaching	14	8.0	2.6	14.4	14	50.0	1.7	34.9
Correctional	80	45.7	5.0	27.8	0	0	0.0	0.0
Support	81	46.3	6.4	35.6	14	50.0	2.8	58.8
Totals	175	100.0	18.0	100.0	28	100.0	4.8	100.0

[a] Computation of CASE II staff time based on employee's duration of affiliation with project and actual work schedule.

20 shows the average number of students assigned per staff member. NTS average daily student population was 245 and for the CASE II project was 25.58. However, in order to compare student load per teaching staff, a weekly NTS academic school of 92 students is used. (Not all NTS inmates attend the academic school; but all CASE II students did.) NTS academic school population figures are based on the average weekly enrollment for the period June 20, 1966, through December 30, 1966. Enrollment data pertinent to the first half of the year is not available.

Table 20. COMPARISON OF AVERAGE NUMBER OF STUDENTS PER STAFF

	Average Number of Students per Staff	
	NTS	CASE II
	(average daily	*(average daily*
Staff Description	*population 245)*	*population 25.58)*
Correctional	3.1	5.1
Full-time teaching	6.6[a]	9.8
All teaching	3.3[a]	5.9
All full-time staff	1.4	1.4
All staff	1.2	1.1

[a] Based on average weekly enrollment at NTS Academic School.

It can be seen that the overall student load per staff was approximately the same for both NTS and CASE II. However, when the student load per teaching staff is compared, the load is seen to be almost twice as much for CASE II when all the teaching staff are considered.

Costs: The February 14, 1967, NTS Fact Sheet indicates total expenditures for that institution during fiscal year 1966 at $1,511,368.00. CASE II expenditures are estimated at $189,788. To make a meaningful comparison between these two figures, several factors are considered. The CASE II expenditures include an NTS estimate for the salaries of the half-time teachers and for the correctional officers provided by that institution. Also, the CASE

II expenditures, in addition to staff salaries and general operating costs, included the cost of materials for the construction of student rooms and offices, the cost of programed materials and machines, texts, and other materials necessary for the establishment of a new curriculum, and purchase of research equipment and materials and equipment for the establishment of the lounge and cafeteria. Certain other purchasing advantages available to the Federal Bureau of Prison facilities—such as institution-grown food and supplied milk, military clothing, and large quantity discount purchasing—were not available to the project.

The average daily cost per student figure for NTS, as stated on the February 14, 1967, Fact Sheet, was sixteen dollars. Several methods can be used to determine a comparative figure for the CASE II project. Table 21 compares these figures with the NTS average daily cost figure. When the actual number of days spent in the project by the students is used as divisor, the average daily cost per CASE II student is twenty-one dollars. However, if this amount is determined on the basis of the daily average CASE II student population, a generally accepted computation method, this average daily cost is reduced to $20.33 (as compared to $16.90 for NTS). A third acceptable method of computing the per student cost of CASE II discounts from total expenses all funds required to renovate the building and purchase the bulk of curriculum materials for the academic program. All other expenses are included in this computation, which is termed "Total, less developmental costs." This results in an average daily cost per student of $18.75. This method seems fair as NTS data on student or institutional costs do not include renovation or construction expenses. It is extremely difficult to compare the costs of an established and operational facility with the costs of a facility which must establish a research operational system. There is little doubt that a project such as CASE II, once it has been established, could maintain its operations at a student cost equivalent to that of the NTS.

The Student Educational Researcher's Handbook

$\bigcirc\bigcirc\bigcirc\bigcirc\bigcirc\bigcirc\bigcirc\bigcirc\bigcirc\bigcirc\bigcirc\bigcirc\bigcirc\bigcirc$

*O*n the first day each student was enrolled in CASE II, he received a copy of a handbook explaining the operations of the project. The following material is a reproduction of the CASE II *Student Educational Researcher Handbook* distributed during the last six months of the project.

FOREWORD

Now that you have completed the basic NTS entrance procedures of photos and fingerprints, haircut, and medical examination, you've arrived at Jefferson Hall. The first step in your stay in this cottage is called orientation.

You have already been introduced to some of the CASE Staff members and, as your first days in CASE go by, you will talk with many more. You will learn how each will work with you in the future. The psychologist, caseworker, chaplain, and the educational coordinator will submit evaluations based on their interviews with you. You will also begin taking many tests during this period. Not only will these tests tell us something of your educational development, but they will also provide you with points, your first earnings in CASE. You will also continue your medical examinations with periodic trips to the hospital.

You will meet a host of new people each of whom, students and staff, can be helpful to your learning of procedures. They will provide a great deal of verbal information on what is going on. This Handbook will also be helpful, and it is hoped that you will consult it regularly. The various categories of information are listed alphabetically in the index. Each major subject heading either tells you the page number that has the information or refers you to another subject heading.

GENERAL INTRODUCTION

Welcome to the CASE II project. Your entrance into Jefferson Hall a short time ago was the beginning of several days of orientation. This introduction to the *Student Educational Researcher Handbook* will attempt to make that beginning easier by answering some of the questions that you might already have. Questions like, what is CASE II and why was I selected? Let's begin with the first question.

CASE II is an educational research project within the National Training School for Boys located here in Washington, D. C. The money for this project comes from two major sources, the Office of Health, Education and Welfare and the Bureau of Prisons. The direct administration and responsibility for CASE II is with an organization called the Institute for Behavorial Research located in Silver Spring, Maryland. This project is the second CASE project here at the National Training School. The original project began in the early spring of 1965 and ran through the fall months. It was similar to this project and much of what was learned during those months has been used to make CASE II. This process of learning how to do things better is really what CASE II is all about.

The word *CASE* is made from the first letters of the four words *Contingencies Applicable* for *Special Education*. What this means is that we, all the CASE II staff members, are looking for better ways to help students learn. So we are all part of a team of lookers, or researchers as they are most often called, and our place of looking is Jefferson Hall.

Why were you selected? The CASE II project needed twenty-eight students representing a cross section of student age and geographic origin typical of the NTS. Only students new to the NTS were to be selected and you were enrolled in the project on a random basis as rapidly as space became available.

Your title as a CASE II student is Student Educational Researcher and as a researcher you will be paid for the work you do for CASE II. Your payment (salary) will be in points. These points can be used just as you would use money. You will be able to pay for a private room, buy your meals, buy clothing, use the lounge, and make purchases from the CASE store. Your position as a Student Educational Researcher will also enable you to take vacations from the National Training School and will hopefully provide you with those academic and social tools which will be valuable to you as a citizen of these United States.

As a Student Educational Researcher you are a free citizen within the project. You will have choices in what you do but your choices will also carry responsibilities. It is the purpose of this *Student Educational Researcher Handbook* to provide an outline of your choices and responsibilities. This *Handbook* is for you to read when you start as a Student Educational Researcher and also to provide a reference for any future questions you may have. However, the *Handbook* is also a part of the CASE II learning process, and it will be changed as we all learn better ways of doing things. When changes are made, you will always be notified.

This *Handbook* is your very first job as Student Educational Researcher with CASE II. About one week from the time of your arrival into CASE II you will be given an orientation test which will tell us how well you understand the procedures of CASE II. You will be expected to pass this test with a grade of 90 per cent or better. But don't become too alarmed. The *Handbook* is only one part of the information and assistance you will be given during the orientation period. You will be interviewed by many of the staff and students and will have CASE II procedures fully explained and

154

hopefully all of your questions answered before you are asked to take the orientation test.

Now that you have some general information about CASE II you can begin to read through the *Handbook*. Don't hesitate to ask any questions that you may have. Remember, we're all learning about learning, and your questions may help us make this *Handbook* better for the next Student Educational Researcher.

Savings Accounts: A minimum of one thousand points shall be required to open an account. Each depositor will receive a deposit book containing a record of his account. Deposits of not less than five hundred points may be received by the bank. Interest shall be payable on balances of 2500 points or more and will be computed on the balance credited on the books for three months at a rate of 5 per cent per annum. Deposits may be made by submitting the account book to the store between 7:00 and 9:00 P.M. Monday through Thursday. The deposit will be reflected in the net points at the time of deposit. The account book, with the deposit recorded, will be returned the following day. Withdrawals of points (moving points from your savings account to your time card) will be negotiated in the same manner during the same time periods. Points will be credited to the store card at the time of withdrawal. The account book will be returned the following day. Withdrawals of cash require seven days' written notice. A service fee of fifty points will be charged to a student who makes a withdrawal from his account before three months from the opening date of the account.

Orientation Loan: This loan is available to all new students during their orientation period. The purpose of this loan is to provide funds (points) for your room, meals, and general purchases until your first regular payday. The maximum amount at present that may be borrowed is 2500 points. These points must be repaid at a minimum rate of two hundred points per week plus 1 per cent interest on the unpaid balance.

Educational Loan: A student may request a loan for purposes of payment of tuition for either educational or vocational

155

classes. Procedures for this loan are generally included in class announcements, or a student may submit a written request to the CASE staff. Generally, an educational loan is one small enough to be repaid in full on the student's next regular payday.

Emergency Loan: A student may make a written request for a loan to cover unexpected expense. A loan of this type is granted only after an evaluation has been made of the student's ability and willingness to work, his general handling of his earnings, and his repayment of any previous loans.

BONUSES

Procedures have been established so that staff members may recommend a bonus (a payment of points or other reward) to a student. The reasons for which a student may receive a bonus may vary from staff member to staff member but are generally on the basis of acceptable social behavior, courtesy, willingness to accept responsibility, and so on. You will be notified in each instance as soon as the bonus has been approved and posted to your store card.

CAFETERIA

The cafeteria is located on the first floor of Jefferson Hall. All of the meals are served at this location. Hours of the meals are listed in the Schedule section of this *Handbook*. Menus for the cafeteria meals are posted so that an SER may know in advance what meals are being offered. Although the cafeteria is fairly small, students and many staff members are served by it daily. Procedures have also been established whereby students may invite their guests (visitors) for Sunday dinner if they wish. With the exception of the weekly evening meals (and for SERs on relief or restriction), SERs may leave the cafeteria after they have finished eating and relax in the lounge.

DRY CLEANING AND ALTERATIONS

Personal clothing that requires dry cleaning or tailored alterations may be dropped off at the store on Saturday. The items will then be taken out for the required work and will normally be available for pick up from the store on the following Saturday. Payment for these services will be made at the time of pick up.

EDUCATIONAL AREA PROCEDURES

The entire second floor, with the exception of the equipment in the storage room on the left hand side of the landing, is used for academic work. This floor will be open for classes and for self-study from Monday through Friday. These are the normal working days of the week. During these times program checkers and teachers will be on duty to help you with your problems. Much of the time you spend on the second floor will be in self-study with programed instructional materials. Certain classes will be offered during these times. Generally, the classes that will be offered during the Monday through Friday hours set aside for school are designed to go hand in hand with the self-instructional programs that you will be studying. Classes will be offered in English, mathematics, social studies, science, and a number of other subject matter areas. At certain times, special interest classes will be offered. For all classes that are offered by CASE, a bulletin will be posted on the board outside in the hall on the second floor. These bulletins will let you know exactly what is required of any student who wishes to take a class.

Student Educational Researchers (SERs) is the name given to students employed by CASE II. Based on orientation testing, interviews, and academic achievement, SERs are placed in one of the following four categories: Level I (freshman), Level II (sophomore), Level III (junior), or Level IV (senior). Each of these levels has three steps, each step based on academic achievement and each one leading upward to the next. Once an SER has completed all requirements for the steps at one level, he is promoted to the next. Programs are assigned a value in points on the basis of these academic levels.

There are a few basic things that each student must know in order to use the second floor in the best way possible. These general guidelines have been set so that each student can rapidly and accurately study his programs, have his programs checked, have points recorded for 90 per cent or better completion of the pro-

157

grams, finish tests on each section of the program studied, and then begin work on a new unit of study.

Checking In for Work: Whenever you come up to the educational floor from either the home floor or the first floor, you must stop at the time clock just inside the double doors and have the staff member on duty punch your time card. When the staff member punches your time card, you are checked in to work. Immediately following your checking in at the time clock, you may go to the program pickup station and pick up your program. The staff member on duty at the program pickup station will punch your pink sheet and you are then able to work directly on your program.

Program Studying: Once you have passed a test on this SER Handbook at a level of 90 per cent or better, you will be given a private office in which you may study your programs and other material that is given to you. Before you have passed the test on this manual, you will do all of your studying on one of the tables in the open space near the program checking station. While studying at either of these two locations, your method of programed study should be the same. The way that you should work with each of the many types of programs that are available to you will be fully explained in advance by a staff member. Once you have begun a unit of any one of these programs, you should answer each question asked of you by the program. Your answers will usually be written on a separate sheet of paper. These answer sheets will always have your name, the date, program and unit, and will be numbered according to the frame or question numbers used in the program. Once you have finished all of the answers in any one unit of a program, check carefully to see that you have not made any errors. At this time you are ready to have your program checked.

Program Checking: When you have completed a unit of your program you should take the unit, your pink sheet, and your completed answer sheet up to the program checking desk. If the teachers or checkers are busy, you should sign your name to the waiting list and place all of your programed materials on the program checker's desk. If the program checkers are not busy, they will check your program immediately. However, if there are a number of programs ahead of yours in the file, you should return to your private office or study area and wait for the program checker to call your name. After your name has been called, you and the checker will together check your program to find out how accurate you have been. If you have done 90 per cent or better on your program, the program checker will briefly review the program with you and will note the points that you have earned on your pink sheet. If you have not done 90 per cent or better on your program, the program checker may require you to do the unit over, redo a portion of the unit again, or do some other work that will aid you in understanding the material. In the case of work done at less than 90 per cent, the program checker will give you explicit directions about what you are to do next. These procedures are listed at the end of this section. For most of the programs that are in service in the CASE project, there is a test which follows every unit of every program. If you have done 90 per cent or better on any unit of the program, you are eligible to take a test covering that unit.

Testing: After you have successfully completed a unit and if there is a test for that unit of the program you were studying, the staff member on duty at the desk will assign you to go directly into the testing room. You will always check with the staff member at the time clock before you leave the area. Upon entrance into the testing room, you will present your assignment sheet to the tester, and the tester will give you a test covering the unit of study which you have just completed. Once you have begun a test in the testing room, you should stay to finish that test. If you do leave while taking any test, you will have that test graded for the amount of work completed, and the score you receive will be considered as a true and accurate record of your knowledge. Once you have completed the test covering the unit, you should quietly take a seat at the tester's checking station and wait until the tester is available to check your test for you. If you have completed your test at 90 per cent or better, the tester will assign you points for that test. If you do not complete a test at 90 per cent or better, you will not earn any points. The tester will make a recommendation on your assignment sheet as to what the teachers or program checkers in the educational area should assign you to do so that you may be able to complete your test at 90 per cent or better. Once the tester has either recorded your points or made his recommendation as to the next bit of work that you should do, you will report to the program checking station. Remember, any disruption in the testing room may cause you to be dismissed from the testing room, thereby losing testing privileges for a specified period of time.

Returning to Study: At the checking station a staff member will check you into your next area of assignment. If you have not successfully completed your testing, the teacher or checker will either give you help or assign you other material to study. The procedures for working through a program are listed at the end of this section. Once you have completed all the units of a program and have completed the post-test on that program, a teacher will assign you a new program on which you may begin work.

Classes: The starting time for classes will be announced at least five minutes before the class actually begins. If you are enrolled in or scheduled to go to the announced class, you should then prepare to go to class. When you are going to enter the classroom, leave your self-study work at the program checking station and have your assignment sheet punched before you enter the classroom. You should go to the main time clock station and have the staff member on duty stamp your time card before going into the classroom. If your time card is not punched, you will not receive any points you may have earned. Remember, it is very critical that you make these classes on time. These are the parts of the study program that will help you understand in greater depth the programed instructional material you have recently studied.

Bathroom: When you have to go to the bathroom at any time that you are on the second floor, you must inform the staff member at the time clock. If the bathroom is not in use you will be given permission to use it. When you come out of the bathroom you must also inform the staff member at the time clock.

Library (free area): When you feel tired, don't go to sleep at your study station. SERs will not be allowed to sleep at their study stations. This is a serious violation of work procedures and can result in fines or in eventual dismissal from your study job. If you are tired or can't study, go to the staff member at the time clock and check out on your time card. The staff member will allow you to go to the library to browse and relax. You are asked to be generally quiet while in the library. Other people in the room are studying. Please respect their study behaviors even though you are not studying yourself. Be sure to have the staff member stamp your time card when you return to studying from the library. If you are checked out of work you are not to wander around the study floor disrupting others while they are studying.

Help and Information: You can ask any staff member on duty for help on any part of your program at any time. The staff member will help you in any way that he or she can. If you are having extreme difficulty with a unit of a program, you should go directly to the teacher most concerned with the subject matter and request help.

Procedures for Working Through a Program: As a Student Educational Researcher, you will receive payment (points) for showing that you have successfully learned the materials that you have been studying. A score of 90 per cent accuracy (or better) indicates to the staff that you have successfully learned your study materials. However, should you achieve below 90 per cent accuracy on either a program check or a test, procedures have been established to aid you in successfully completing a unit or test and to aid the staff in assisting and evaluating your progress. These procedures are indicated in the flow charts in the educational area and are written out for you here.

There are eight major steps and seven substeps in the procedure for completing a program. You begin step 1 when you receive your program assignment and, as you can see on the flow chart, you will be able to work right through the eight steps if you perform at 90 per cent or better accuracy. If you should fall below the 90 per cent level, then your progress will be directed through the substeps. Each of these substeps indicates what you must do in order to get back into the major step progress through your program.

161

A New Learning Environment

Step 1—Program Assignment.

Step 2—Program Work.

Step 3—Program Check. (If required 90 per cent or better, then go to step 4.)

Substep 3a—If 85 per cent to 90 per cent accurate: You will be given a verbal or written review or help session with the teacher or checker. If the staff member is satisfied with the review then you will go to step 4. If you are not able to successfully demonstrate your knowledge of the unit, you will go to substep 3c.

Substep 3b—You will be given a verbal or written review or help session with the teacher or checker. If the staff member is satisfied you will go to substep 5a. If not satisfied you will go to substep 3c.

Substep 3c—Less than 85 per cent accurate or unsatisfactory with substeps 3a, 3b, 7a or 7b. The student must be reassigned unit, part of unit, test frames, or other related study materials. Use of this substep automatically recycles the student to step 1.

Step 4—Program Point Assignment.

Substep 4a—If no test exists the student goes to step 1.

Step 5—Test Assignment.

Substep 5a—Retake of test using alternate form.

Step 6—Test Take.

Step 7—Test Check.

Substep 7a—If 85 per cent to 90 per cent accurate on first test take. A verbal check or help session is required. If the tester is satisfied that the student's minor difficulties have been resolved, the student goes to substep 5a. If the tester is dissatisfied the student goes to substep 3b.

Substep 7b—Below 85 per cent accuracy on first test take or below 90 per cent on alternate. Student goes to substep 3c.

Step 8—Test Points Assignment.

When a student's behavior is such that some means of discipline is required, a staff member may recommend that a fine (a loss of points or loss of privilege) be effected. Fines are divided into two categories, major fines and minor fines. The minor fines are those from one to ninety-nine points. These fines will not affect a student's privileges such as shopping trips, town trips, leaves, furloughs, telephone calls, and so on. Minor fines can be issued for the lack of proper clothing, minor horseplay, and fighting in defense of person. Major fines are those starting at one hundred points. These fines will affect a student's privileges and can be issued for assault on person or property, agitation, constant horseplay, constant use of vulgar and abusive language, disruption in the educational area, cheating, and smoking after lights out. The fine areas listed above are not to be considered all inclusive and final. They are rather to be considered as typical examples. Remember that the many privileges granted to an SER go hand in hand with his responsibilities. An SER's regard for CASE rules and regulations is an important factor in the privileges that are made available to him. Should a student feel that he has been unjustly fined he may submit a letter to the Committee for Student Affairs to that effect. All such letters should thoroughly mention all circumstances of the incident and present reasons why the fine should be altered or removed.

INTERVIEWS

CASE students are interviewed by the staff periodically. However, if a student has a particular problem or wishes counsel about a personal matter, he may request an interview with a CASE II staff member of his choice. Staff members have a request for interview form which will be filled out at the time a student requests the interview. Once the appointment has been confirmed with the staff member the student wishes to see, the student will be notified of the time, date, and cost (if any).

JEFFERSON HALL

The CASE II Building, Jefferson Hall, contains four floors. Each floor has different features and different uses. The ground floor, called the home floor, is a kind of dormitory. It is divided into private rooms containing a bed, chair, lamp, file cabinet, and closet/desk unit. The shower room, major bathroom, and an open sleeping area for relief students are also found on this floor. The first floor contains the CASE II administrative offices, the lounge and the store, and the kitchen and cafeteria. The third floor contains the CASE II teaching staff offices, an interview room, rooms that will be used for shop or craft courses, and a photographic dark room.

LAUNDRY SERVICES

An automatic washer is located in the bathroom on the home floor. (See Schedules for the hours this machine is available for use.) The procedures for use of the washing machine are as follows: When a student wishes to use the washing machine, he will sign up with the home floor officer. When the washing machine is available, the home floor officer will notify the student next on the sign up list. The student will check out of the home floor for the CASE store and will purchase a Washing Machine Rental Slip. He will return to the home floor with the Rental Slip and present it to the home floor officer. The home floor officer will take the Rental Slip, initial it, and stamp it on the time clock. He will then tell the student that he can load his laundry into the washing machine. When the machine is loaded, the student will inform the officer and the officer will insert the quarter into the machine and check to insure the start of the washing cycle. When the student is finished with the machine, he will inform the officer so that the next student on the list can be called.

LEAVES

After four months of residency in the CASE project, a student will be considered as eligible to make a request for either a shopping trip or a sponsored leave. (*Note:* All applications for shopping trips or leaves must be submitted to the CSA—Committee for Student Affairs—at least ten days prior to the intended date of leave.) Following are the requirements for these and the additional trips from CASE.

Shopping Trips: These trips are to be for no more than three hours in length and will be made at local stores or shopping centers selected by the staff. Due to staff time restrictions, only two students will be permitted per trip and a postponement of the trip will be made should no staff be available. The SER must have at least a 2500 point bank balance to be used for purchases. He must have had no major fine for four weeks prior to the shopping date. If this is not the first shopping trip, the date requested must be at least four weeks after the previous shopping trip. (*Note:* A shopping trip with a CASE staff member may be counted as *one* of the escorted leaves—this is for Federal SERs only.)

Escorted and Unescorted Leaves: After the four month

residency requirement, there are five general requirements which must be fulfilled in order to be eligible for either type of leave. These are: (1) Have a good academic progress record for at least the four weeks prior to the date of leave. (These progress reports are made by the teaching staff.) (2) Have a good record of social behaviors in all areas of the project for at least four weeks prior to the date of leave. (These behavior reports are gathered from the correctional officers, teaching assistants, and other staff members.) (3) Have had no major fine or other disciplinary action for at least the four weeks prior to the date of leave. (This is reviewed by the Committee for Student Affairs.) (4) Have enough points to pay for any public transportation used for the travel. (5) Have a minimum of five hundred points for each day spent on leave. This will be your spending money.

Escorted Leaves: First Leave: This trip will be allowed on either a Saturday or Sunday, from 10:00 a.m. to 8:00 p.m. The SER shall be picked up and returned by his parent, guardian, or sponsor. (*Note:* An SER whose parents or guardians live outside of the District of Columbia may make application for this leave and request that CASE provide a sponsor. The hours of a sponsored trip may vary slightly from those stated above and will be arranged on a basis of staff convenience. Second Leave: Four calendar weeks from the date of Leave #1 an SER is eligible for Leave #2. The requirements for and length of this leave are the same as for Leave #1. (*Note:* A shopping trip with a CASE staff member may be counted as one of the two escorted leaves—this is for Federal SERs only.)

Unescorted Leaves (after a six month residency in the CASE Project and successful completion of Leaves #1 and #2): Third Leave: Four calendar weeks from the date of Leave #2, the SER will be eligible for Leave #3. This leave will be unescorted and will be either forty-eight or seventy-two hours in length. The length will be decided by the CSA. (*Note:* A Federal student who wishes to make an unescorted leave in the District of Columbia can make application for such. However, the length and conditions of the leave will be arranged by the CSA.) Fourth Leave: Two calendar

165

weeks from the date of Leave #3 the SER is eligible for Leave #4. This leave will be under the same conditions as Leave #3. After successfully completing Leave #4, a student will be eligible to make application for additional leaves. Leaves requested after Leave #4 until the date of parole will be arranged by the Committee for Student Affairs.

Absent Without Leave: Students that fail to return from an authorized trip or that absent themselves from Jefferson Hall without authorization will come under the following conditions upon return to Jefferson Hall: (1) A condition of probation will be in effect for one month. (2) A #1 Room Restriction will be imposed for at least five working days commencing with the day following the return to Jefferson Hall. (3) During the one month probationary period all mail and visiting privileges will be removed with the exception of mail to and from the immediate family and visits by the immediate family. (4) All point earnings and all possessions will be confiscated. These can be regained on a schedule that will be provided by the CSA. (5) Earned good time may be withheld. (6) Students will be considered as new students with a new project entry date. (7) Private office privileges will be revoked until such time as all debts that may have been incurred are paid. (8) A student will not be allowed to go on relief until all debts are paid. *Note:* Final decision about these conditions and any others rests with the CSA.

LIBRARY

The CASE library/seminar-classroom is located in the educational area on the second floor. (See Schedules section of this manual for the hours.) At present there is no fee for using the library/seminar-classroom. Books, magazines, and other materials are available for use in the library. Specific information concerning the loan of reference materials is available from the staff. Special television programs and newscasts are scheduled for showing to library patrons. Notice of these and other bulletins are posted in the educational area. The staff will gladly assist you in selecting books, either for enjoyment or ones that will assist you in your school work. As a part of the library service, there are paperback book racks in the library, in the lounge and on the home floor. These books are available for your use while you are a member of CASE. They were selected by both the students and staff for this purpose. The only restriction on the use of these books is that students are requested to take no more than four or five books from the racks at any one time and to return the books when you are finished with them.

LOUNGE

The CASE lounge is located on the first floor of Jefferson Hall and is the major indoor recreation area. (See Schedules in this *Handbook* for the lounge hours and costs.) It contains a pool table, pingpong table, juke box, and coke machine. Use of these items is secured through the storekeeper. Also, playing cards, games, and other items can be rented for use in the lounge. Aside from the rentals that are available, the lounge is the area from which most purchases are made. The lounge provides a visiting area for family and other guests. It is also the area for general social activities.

MAIL PROCEDURES

Student Educational Researchers are permitted to correspond with people other than their families, such as girl friends, buddies, and so on. However, a requirement is that each person that a student wishes to write must be listed on a visitor/correspondent sheet. (These sheets are available on the home floor.) For people that you wish to write that are not of your immediate family, you must indicate the name and address of the correspondent's parents.

Incoming student mail is delivered by the afternoon correctional officer to CASE. This mail is then xeroxed (a copy is made of both the incoming and outgoing mail) and read by the correctional officer or supervisory staff member prior to delivery. Normally, the student will receive his mail shortly after the evening meal.

When a student wishes to send a letter out, he may pick up an envelope from the officer on the home floor. It is important that the student place his name on the *inside* of the envelope flap. He should also be sure that he has the person to whom he is writing listed on his visitor/correspondent sheet.

A New Learning Environment

After the letter is written, it must be placed, unsealed, in the box on the home floor. All outgoing mail is checked against the student's visitor/correspondent list, read, and a xerox copy made before it is taken down to the NTS mailroom. Letters written and deposited in the outgoing mailbox on the home floor will generally be out to the post office the following afternoon. SERs are not permitted to receive gifts except on their birthdays and at Christmas time. The content of all outgoing student mail is the responsibility of the SER. However, a general rule about language usage is that it should be printable in one of the Washington, D. C., newspapers. Disregard of this may result in a letter's return to the SER.

MEDICAL AND DENTAL SERVICES

Basic medical and dental services are furnished to CASE Student Educational Researchers without cost. If a student has a medical or dental problem, he should inform the home floor officer early in the morning so that he can go on sick call at 8:00 A.M. Emergency medical aid is available when it is needed. Psychological and psychiatric services are available, by appointment, to a student should he desire them. An appointment for these services may be made through any staff member and a student will be informed of both the cost and appointment time. Should a student desire medical or dental attention of a special nature, he should make a request in writing to the CASE staff and arrangements, if possible, will be made.

MOVIES

A weekly Saturday night movie is scheduled. The exact time of the movie and the cost are listed under Schedule in the *Handbook*. Films are also shown periodically in conjunction with classes and at other times. Notices of these films will be posted on the CASE bulletin boards.

MUSIC

Students may purchase or rent musical instruments if they so desire. All transactions of this type will be handled by the store.

If necessary, arrangements will be made for a practice area for musical instruments or singing groups. CASE students are also invited to participate in the NTS choir. If a student wishes to join the choir, he should write a request to the chaplain or a member of the CASE staff.

OUTDOOR ACTIVITIES

Shortly after you arrive at Jefferson Hall you will receive clearance from the NTS Hospital (the completion of your entrance examination and shots). Once this clearance has been received you will be eligible to join in the outdoor activities.

The outdoor activity periods vary with the seasonal weather conditions and currently the following procedures are in effect: (1) The hours for outside recreation will be approximately 4:00–5:00 P.M. (2) The recreation period will take place on Monday, Wednesday, Thursday, and Friday. (3) Any student who wishes to join this outside group must sign up at the time clock on the educational floor *before* 4:00 P.M. (4) An officer will be at the educational floor time clock station at 4:00 P.M. and will take the students outside.

Outdoor activity periods are also held on weekends at various hours. The home floor officer will inform the students of these times. Generally, the outdoor activities are basketball, ball playing, horseshoes, and other games. CASE II students are also invited to participate in organized NTS sports events on holidays.

When the weather permits, all students who attend the outdoor activities are encouraged to wear shorts, either the issue khaki or personally purchased ones. While outside, students are to remain in the area immediately in front of Jefferson Hall (this is the area including the basketball court and the field area between Jefferson Hall and Franklin Hall). During the winter period, Sunday, Tuesday and Wednesday evenings are scheduled gym activities times. If you wish to go you should sign up with the home floor officer.

PAROLE PROCEDURES

Shortly after your arrival at CASE II you will be interviewed by your case worker. He will explain parole procedures to you. He will also periodically schedule interviews with you, but, if you should desire to see him between these periods you may make an appointment to do so. He should be consulted if you have any questions concerning your parole.

Your eligibility for parole is based on many factors within the CASE II project. Reports of your daily social and academic behaviors are reviewed by your case worker. These reports are written by the general project, teaching and administrative staff members. The CASE II administrative staff meets weekly with your case worker and a review, based on your daily behavior reports, is made to determine your eligibility for parole.

PAYROLL PROCEDURES

The section of the CASE II project called data control and banking is responsible for recording information on your earnings and spendings and other activities relative to the research project. Each week, on Friday, you will receive a record of those activities that relate to your financial status. That record, or payroll form, will provide the following information.

Date: Payroll period, Friday A.M. through Thursday P.M.

Previous Net: Points from previous Friday payroll after deductions.

Points Spent: Total points spent during the week since payday.

Balance: Points remaining at the end of the payroll period, that is, Thursday p.m. These points are carried forward to the next week.

Previous Net, Points Spent, and *Balance* will provide you with a copy of the information on our records. It will assist you in balancing your financial books.

Programs, Tests, Classes: Points earned for programed instruction and related activities.

Employment: Number of hours recorded on time cards and pay rate for job. For students with jobs only.

Gross Pay: Total points earned from programs, tests and classes, and employment added to balance of points remaining from previous payroll.

Deposit for Meals: Payment of the minimum required deposit for weekly meals. A larger amount will be deducted if you so indicate on Thursday evening.

Loans: Payment on the loan received at the beginning of the project. Payment will include 1 per cent interest on unpaid balance.

Room Plan: Payment for type of room requested Thursday evening.

Others: Will encompass such categories as regular savings deductions, bank purchases, and the like.

Total Deductions: Sum of points subtracted to meet living expenses.

Net Pay: Points remaining when total deductions are subtracted from gross pay. Net pay represents spending available for the coming week.

Using this information—especially the final figure, net pay—you will be expected to maintain an accurate record of your expenditures in order to keep within the limits of your net points. Ledgers will be available in the store to aid you in setting up a budget of your expenses.

PHONE CALLS

Students wishing to make a phone call to their parents will observe the following regulations: A student must have received *no major fines* or *disciplinary action* for *two weeks* prior to the Friday of the requested call. A request for phone call form will be filled out completely and turned in to the home floor officer. The officer will initial it, stamp the time received, and deposit it in the Committee for Student Affairs Box in the office by Friday, 8 A.M. The student will be notified Friday evening if his application has been approved. Calls will be made on Friday evening no earlier than 8 P.M., and will be limited to three minutes in length. The student will be assigned a time to report to the officer supervising the calls. The request forms of completed calls will be turned in to the storekeeper by the officer when all calls have been finished. The cost of the call will be deducted on Friday. Please list the cost of the call on the request form.

A New Learning Environment

Location	Cost	Location	Cost
Alabama	100	Nebraska	150
Arizona	175	Nevada	200
Arkansas	125	New Hampshire	100
California	200	New Jersey	75
Colorado	175	New Mexico	175
Connecticut	100	New York	75
Delaware	75	North Carolina	75
Florida	100	North Dakota	150
Georgia	100	Ohio	100
Idaho	175	Oklahoma	150
Illinois	100	Oregon	200
Indiana	100	Pennsylvania	75
Iowa	125	Rhode Island	100
Kansas	150	South Carolina	100
Kentucky	100	South Dakota	150
Louisiana	125	Tennessee	100
Maine	100	Texas	150
Maryland	75	Utah	175
Massachusetts	100	Vermont	100
Michigan	100	Virginia	75
Minnesota	125	Washington	200
Mississippi	100	West Virginia	75
Missouri	125	Wisconsin	100
Montana	175	Wyoming	175
District of Columbia & Metropolitan Area	25	Annapolis, Baltimore	50

PRIVATE SHOWERS

Three private shower stalls are located within the shower room on the home floor. These private showers are available for rental by any CASE student who so desires. Rental of one of these showers can be made on your room/meal request slip. One of the advantages of the private shower is that, in addition to being able to shower during the normal showering hours, he can shower later in the evening. See Schedules in this Handbook for costs and shower hours.

RELEASE PROGRAMS

At the present time procedures are being developed whereby students will be able to attend a local school or take part-time employment. This means that a student will live at CASE II (Jefferson Hall) and be able to travel to school or work each day. Application forms for school and work release programs are available on the home floor. In order to be eligible a student must have at least four months' residency in CASE II and be of a junior or senior academic rank.

RELIEF STATUS

Should a student indicate on his room/meal request that he wishes to go on relief (or should a student have insufficient funds), he will be placed on relief starting Friday. As of Friday A.M. all earnings will be frozen until such time as a student removes himself from relief status. (A student will not be able to request removal from a relief status until the following Thursday when the room/meal requests are available.) This means that a student cannot spend any of his points until such time as he has moved back into his private room. All of the points a student may earn during the period he is on relief will remain in a separate account and will never be converted into United States currency. These points will be used only for CASE services and purchases of items that are available as stock items in the store. (What this means is that all the points that a student earns during his relief period cannot be used for travel expenses, shopping trips, catalog orders, or any other function where points are to be converted into United States currency. If these points have not been spent prior to his leaving the CASE project, they will be lost.)

Relief students will be provided a place to sleep and will be issued meals. Your clothing will be issued to you on the normal issue days and you will be required to wear this issued clothing and maintain a neat appearance. Each morning you will be awakened prior to your breakfast with enough time to get dressed, make your individual beds (with collar), clean the area around your bunk, wash and shave. You will be given adequate, nutritional food on metal trays. You will have no selection or choice in the food. You will eat your meals on the home floor. At 10:00 P.M., the home floor officer will give notice of the hour and you will be required to go to your bed and retire for the night.

A New Learning Environment

Relief students will be issued cigarettes by the officer, four per day. Relief students may have visitors at Jefferson Hall during the normal Sunday visiting hours. However, visitors will be restricted to the student's immediate family, be restricted to the entrance hall, be here for only one-half hour. A student who has had prior rental of a private room will be required to place all of his personal belongings, with the exception of minimum toilet articles (specific items to be decided by the officer), in storage until such time as the student removes himself from relief status. Students on relief are restricted to the area immediately near their bunk. They may not visit with other students in their rooms. Relief students will be required to shower daily at the officer's convenience.

Should a student indicate on his room/meal request that he wishes to remove himself from relief (and if he has sufficient funds to do so), he will be released from relief status Friday morning at which time his points will be unfrozen and he can regain a private room. His regular meals in the cafeteria will begin with breakfast Friday morning. A student on relief will have his previously rented room held for him for one week. If he fails to come off relief after one week his room may be requested by another student.

RELIGIOUS SERVICES

Sunday services are available for all CASE students at the NTS chapel. See Schedules in this Handbook for a listing of the hours. In addition to the scheduled Sunday services, CASE is visited regularly by the NTS chaplain and the Catholic priest. CASE students are also encouraged to participate in the NTS choir. Appointments can be made by students for an interview with Chaplain Summer or Father Toohey. These interviews will be at a cost of twenty-five points per fifteen minutes. Sunday evening programs held in the NTS chapel will be available at a cost of fifteen points per evening. All fees paid for religious services will be donated to a charity of your choice.

RESTRICTION

When a student's behaviors are such that some drastic disciplinary action is necessary, the student may be placed on restriction. Following is an outline of the types of restrictions that will be imposed on students for behaviors unacceptable to the students and staff. Restriction #1: Room restriction with no privileges. Restriction #2: Room restriction with some privileges. Restriction #3: Home floor restriction without privileges. Restriction #4: Home floor restriction with some privileges.

Specific Listing of Restrictions by Type:

	Restriction #1	#2	#3	#4
Assignment to a room under home floor officer's observation	X			
Restriction to room	X	X		
Restriction to home floor			X	X
Permission to attend educational area at normal hours	X	X	X	X
Restriction on use of all points	X		X	
Permission to purchase cigarettes and toilet articles		X		X
Meals on the home floor upon metal trays	X	X	X	
Meals in the cafeteria at normal time				X
Mail restricted to only the immediate family	X	X		
No Sunday visitors	X		X	
Sunday visits for one-half hour with immediate family		X		X
Permission to use evening educational area if approved				X
Permission to use evening library area				X
Must request permission to use bathroom and shower	X			
No receipt of any articles or materials from anyone	X	X		

NOTE: A restriction of any type is considered a major fine and will affect the student's privileges accordingly. Any student aiding or attempting to aid a student on restriction in violation of that student's restrictions will be issued major disciplinary action.

A New Learning Environment

The home floor contains twenty-eight private rooms which are available for rental by CASE students. These rooms contain a bed, lockable cabinet, and lamp. The lockable cabinet door opens and provides a desk surface. These rooms allow you an area of privacy and provide a place for your personal belongings, pictures, and so on. The walls may be decorated with photos and pictures provided that the pictures are either those of your family and friends or were acquired from materials purchased through the CASE store. Furniture and other items not supplied with the base rental price of the room may be purchased and/or rented from the store. SERs are responsible for their own awakening time each morning. After the SER arises each morning, he may wash and dress at his own convenience. However, he must leave the home floor at its closing time.

A Student Educational Researcher should take pride in his personal appearance and show individual responsibility. As a guide, you will be required to wear the following when you leave the home floor. You must have on a shirt and trousers. These may be either NTS issue or your own personally purchased items. You must wear socks with either shoes or clogs. Shirts, with tails, must be tucked in. A neat and well groomed appearance is definitely to your advantage. SERs will be totally responsible for the cleanliness of their individual rooms. An SER will be expected to maintain his room with some degree of concern and he will be notified should he fail to meet a minimum of cleanliness.

An SER is expected to respect the privacy of another SER's room and should visit only when invited. It is important to remember that an SER is to return to his individual room after the lights out period. If he desires to stay awake he may do so but must respect the rights of other SERs who may desire to go to sleep. Due to the possible fire hazard, SERs are not permitted to smoke in their rooms after lights out. Should an urgent need be felt for smoking, an SER may request permission to sit near the officer's desk for a smoke break. Should an individual SER be placed on restriction, it is the

176

responsibility of every other SER to respect that status. SERs who fail to do so may find themselves in a similar status.

An SER must check out of and into each station's time clock. In other words, when an SER leaves the home floor, he must first tell the home floor officer or staff member that he is checking out. Then, (for example) when he arrives at the store, he must tell the staff member working there that he is checking in. This checking in and out is very essential for research purposes and is one of the prime responsibilities of an SER.

Boisterous and noisy behavior should be confined to outdoor or gym activities. Remember, in closed quarters a small amount of noise travels a great distance! SERs will not be permitted to bring bottled soft drinks into the private rooms or into the home floor. Foodstuff items will be permitted in the private rooms provided they are kept stored in a sealed metal or plastic container.

Should a student desire to change his room location or desire to make modifications to a room, the following procedures will be observed. A request for room change will be written and addressed to the senior CASE correctional officer and must contain the following information: the reason for the room change request; the number of the room presently occupied; the number of the room desired; if necessary, a specific listing of modifications desired; signature of all parties involved. *Note:* Room modifications will generally require a deposit which will be determined after a cost/labor analysis of the requested modification. Changes that are approved will result in notice given to the student submitting the request and will state the time and date they will be effected.

SCHEDULES

CAFETERIA:

Monday thru Friday

Breakfast—Serving hours:

Freshmen	7:30 A.M.– 7:45 A.M.
Sophomores	7:45 A.M.– 7:50 A.M.
Juniors and Seniors	7:50 A.M.– 8:00 A.M.

Cafeteria closes at 8:15 A.M.

A New Learning Environment

Lunch—Serving hours:

Seniors and Juniors .... 12:00 P.M.–12:15 P.M.
Sophomores .... 12:15 P.M.–12:30 P.M.
Freshmen .... 12:30 P.M.–12:45 P.M.
　　Cafeteria closes at 1:00 P.M.

Supper—Serving hours:

Seniors and Juniors .... 5:00 P.M.– 5:10 P.M.
Sophomores .... 5:10 P.M.– 5:20 P.M.
Freshmen .... 5:20 P.M.– 5:30 P.M.
　　Cafeteria closes at 5:45 P.M.

Saturday

Breakfast—Serving hours:

Freshmen .... 8:30 A.M.– 8:40 A.M.
Sophomores .... 8:40 A.M.– 8:50 A.M.
Juniors and Seniors .... 8:50 A.M.– 9:00 A.M.
　　Cafeteria closes at 9:15 A.M.

Lunch—Serving hours:

Seniors and Juniors .... 12:00 P.M.–12:15 P.M.
Sophomores .... 12:15 P.M.–12:30 P.M.
Freshmen .... 12:30 P.M.–12:45 P.M.
　　Cafeteria closes at 1:00 P.M.

Sunday

Breakfast—Serving hours:

All students .... 10:00 A.M.–11:00 A.M.
　　Cafeteria closes at 11:15 A.M.

Dinner—Serving hours:

Students with paid dinner guests ... 3:00 P.M.– 3:30 P.M.
All other students .... 3:30 P.M.– 4:30 P.M.
　　Cafeteria closes at 4:45 P.M.

NOTE: Students will indicate a deposit for their weekly meals on the room/meal request on Thursday evening.

Church Services: Both Catholic and Protestant services are held on Sundays at 9:45 A.M. There is no cost for attendance. If a student desires to attend services he should inform the home floor officer on Sunday morning.

Educational Area Hours: The educational area is open daily,

Monday through Thursday, from 8:30 A.M. until 11:45 A.M. and from 1:30 P.M. until 4:30 P.M. On Friday the area is open from 8:30 A.M. until 11:45 A.M. and from 1:30 P.M. until 3:30 P.M. The area is also open in the evening, Monday through Friday, between the hours of 6:30 P.M. and 9:30 P.M. Students wishing to use the area during the evening hours should use the request form provided on the educational floor.

Special evening or daytime hours may be scheduled for classes or television showings. These special hours will always be posted and opportunity given to the student to avail himself.

Laundry Hours and Costs: Monday thru Friday—6:00 P.M.–10:00 P.M. Saturday and Sunday—8:00 A.M.–10:00 P.M. The cost of the machine is twenty-five points per load. Procedures for using the machine are explained in the Laundry Services section of this handbook.

Library Hours: The CASE II Library is normally open Monday through Friday from 6:30 P.M. to 9:30 P.M. It is not normally open on Saturday and Sunday. Special hours may be arranged to accommodate special television showings or other events. There is no cost for use of the library.

Rooms, Student: Students desiring to rent a private room may do so by indicating such on the weekly room/meal request form each Thursday evening. Cost of the room is 800 points per week. A discount rental of 200 points is offered every fifth consecutive week of rental.

Seminar: A student seminar is scheduled each Friday from 5:45 to 6:15 P.M. in the educational area.

Showers, Private: Cost of 200 points/week. Hours: 6:00 P.M.—10:00 P.M. (no time limit); 10:00 P.M.—12:00 midnight (15 minute time limit).

Store Hours: Sunday—1:00 P.M.–9:30 P.M. Monday–Friday—6:00 P.M.–9:30 P.M. Saturday—1:00 P.M.–10:00 P.M. (all major purchases, rentals, dry cleaning, etc.).

Visiting Hours: Sunday—1:00 P.M.–4:00 P.M. Special hours may be arranged for out-of-town visitors.

179

Lounge Hours and Costs:

Hours	Sun.	Mon.	Tues.	Wed.	Thurs.	Fri.	Sat.
1:00 P.M.–2:00 P.M.	Free	Closed	Closed	Closed	Closed	Closed	25 pts.
2:00 P.M.–3:00 P.M.	Free	Closed	Closed	Closed	Closed	Closed	25 pts.
3:00 P.M.–4:00 P.M.	10 pts.	100 pts.	100 pts.	100 pts.	100 pts.	100 pts.	25 pts.
4:00 P.M.–5:00 P.M.	10 pts.	100 pts.	100 pts.	100 pts.	100 pts.	100 pts.	25 pts.
5:00 P.M.–6:00 P.M.	10 pts.	Closed	Closed	Closed	Closed	Closed	25 pts.
6:00 P.M.–6:30 P.M.	10 pts.	Closed	Closed	Closed	Closed	Closed	25 pts.
6:30 P.M.–7:00 P.M.	10 pts.						25 pts.
7:00 P.M.–8:00 P.M.	10 pts.						
8:00 P.M.–	10 pts. until 10:00 P.M.		25 pts. until 10:00 P.M.			50 pts. until 11:00 P.M.	

All of your points, your earnings, spendings, and savings are recorded at the store. The store also is the place that records entrance to the cafeteria and the lounge. You must always check with the staff member when entering or leaving the first floor.

The store carries a stock of items such as paper, pencils, magazines, Cokes, candy, cigarettes, soap, and so on. It also has catalogs from which a student may select items for purchase. Salesmen are periodically called in to present their wares to the students. Items which are not offered by the store or catalog may be purchased by a student on his authorized shopping trip.

Washing machine rental slips and Saturday night movie tickets are also purchased in the store. Special sales are occasionally held, and notice of these and other events are posted in the store. If you have any additional questions you may ask the storekeeper. *Note:* Students who wish to make store purchases but do not want to go into the lounge may do so Monday through Friday from 6:00 P.M. until 6:30 P.M. At all other times a student must pay the lounge entrance fee.

STUDENT WORKERS

CASE II employs some SERs as part-time workers. Generally, these students work in the evening or during other nonschool time at various jobs. Some jobs currently handled by student help are general clean-up, janitorial, general clerical, bus boy, and food preparation assistant. Wages are paid either on an hourly or unit basis depending on the task. Students are offered these jobs on the basis of their abilities and willingness to accept responsibilities as indicated by both their social and academic behavior.

TIME CARDS

You will find that you have at least three daily time cards. These cards will be located at the time clocks on the home floor, in the store, and on the educational floor. These cards are a very important part of your record as a CASE student. For example, the time card located in the store contains information concerning your earnings and daily spendings. The card on the educational floor contains information concerning your daily earnings and work time. Without the information on this card, you could not be paid on pay day or credited with leave or sick time. Time cards are also used to keep a record of the work time of the part-time student workers.

TIME CLOCKS

At the present time CASE II has four time clocks. These clocks are located on the home floor, in the store and on the educational floor. Along with an SER's time card, these clocks provide valuable information concerning the day's activities within CASE II. Each time the clock is used to imprint a time card, it automatically records the day, hour, and minute. It is hardly necessary to say that these clocks are costly, precision machines and are to be used only by members of the CASE II staff.

VISITORS

SERs are normally allowed visitors on Sunday afternoons (see Schedules for visiting hours in this Handbook). Families and friends are able to visit at CASE II providing the SER has placed them on his visitor/correspondent list. Visitors may be invited to be an SER's guest for the Sunday afternoon meal. Special visiting hours can be arranged for out-of-town visitors should they arrive at a time other than Sunday.

An SER may not accept gifts from visitors except at Christmas time or on his birthday. The responsibility for this belongs to the SER. Visitors are generally not allowed to tour the CASE II building and should remain either in the lounge or on the Jefferson Hall front porch. If you wish to have your visitors as Sunday dinner guests you must inform Mr. Hamilton (cafeteria manager) on the Friday prior to the Sunday you wish to have the dinner guests. Costs for the meal(s) will be deducted at this time.

VOCATIONAL CLASSES

Vocational classes are offered periodically to CASE II SERs. Usually these classes are held during the evening hours. Subjects for the classes range from typing to electronics.

Notice of any new class is posted on the bulletin board outside of the educational area. These notices list the requirements if any, hours, costs, and so on. SERs wishing to enroll in any of these classes may do so providing they are able to meet the requirements. Procedures for enrolling will always be posted on the class notice.

References

AYLLON, T., AND AZRIN, N. "The Measurement and Reinforcement of Behavior of Psychotics." *Journal of the Experimental Analysis of Behavior,* 1965, *8.*

COHEN, H. L. "Behavioral Architecture." *Architectural Association Journal,* London, June 1964.

COHEN, H. L. "Designing Educational Environments for Institutional Adolescents." Invited address presented at the American Psychological Association Annual Meeting, August 31 to September 4, 1969.

COHEN, H. L. "Educational Therapy." In J. Meltzoff and M. Kornreich, *Research in Psychotherapy.* New York: Atherton, 1968.

COHEN, H. L. "In Support of Human Behavior." *Art Education,* October 1969.

COHEN, H. L., FILIPCZAK, J., AND BIS, J. S. *CASE I: An Initial Study of Contingencies Applicable to Special Education.* Silver Spring, Md.: Educational Facility Press—IBR, 1967.

COHEN, H. L., FILIPCZAK, J., BIS, J., COHEN, J., GOLDIAMOND, I., AND LARKIN, P. *CASE II—MODEL: A Contingency Oriented Twenty-Four-Hour Learning Environment in a Juvenile Correctional Institution.* Silver Spring, Md.: IBR Press, 1968.

COHEN, H. L., GOLDIAMOND, I., FILIPCZAK, J., AND POOLEY, R. *Training Professionals in Procedures for the Establishment of Educational Environments.* Silver Spring, Md.: IBR Press, 1968.

COHEN, H. L., KIBLER, R., AND MILES, D. A. "A Preliminary Report on a Pilot Study for Educating Low Achievers." *Inter-University Committee on the Superior Student Journal,* 1964, *6.*

FERSTER, C., AND DE MEYER, M. "A Method for the Experimental Anal-

185

References

ysis of the Behavior of Autistic Children." *American Journal of Orthopsychiatry*, 1962, *32*.

GLASER, D. *The Effectiveness of a Prison and Parole System*. Indianapolis: Bobbs-Merrill, 1964.

GOLDIAMOND, I., AND DYRUD, J. E. "Some Applications and Implications of Behavioral Analysis for Psychotherapy." *Research in Psychotherapy*, 1968, *3*.

LEVINSON, R. "A Report on the Demonstration Counseling Project." Unpublished report, Federal Bureau of Prisons, 1965.

LITWACK, L. "An Examination of Ten Significant Differences Between Juvenile Recidivists and Nonrecidivists." *Journal of Educational Research*, 1961, *LV*.

LITWACK, L. "Prediction of Recidivism among Juvenile Delinquents." *Journal of Educational Research*, 1967, *LXI*.

LOVAAS, O. I., BERBERICH, J. P., PERLOFF, B. F., AND SCHAEFFER, B. "Acquisition of Imitative Speech by Schizophrenic Children." *Science*, 1966, *151*, 705–707.

LUMSDAINE, A., AND GLASER, R. *Teaching Machines and Programmed Learning: A Source Book*. Washington: Department of Audio-Visual Instruction, National Education Association, 1960.

MC KEGNEY, F. P. "A Baseline Expectancy Study at the National Training School for Boys." Unpublished report, Federal Bureau of Prisons, 1963.

OHLIN, L. E. *Selection for Parole: A Manual for Parole Prediction*. New York: Russell Sage Foundation, 1951.

PREMACK, D. "Toward Empirical Behavior Laws: I.—Positive Reinforcement." *Psychological Review*, 1959, *66*.

PRESSEY, S. L. "A Simple Device for Teaching, Testing, and Research in Learning." *School and Society*, 1926, *23*.

SIDMAN, M., AND STODDARD, L. "Programing Perception and Learning for Retarded Children." *International Review of Research in Mental Retardation*, 1966, *2*.

SKINNER, B. F. *The Technology of Teaching*. New York: Appleton-Century-Crofts, 1968.

Index

A

Absent without leave (AWOL), 33, 166
Academic failure, reasons for, 2–3
Academic program, 3–4, 9, 11, 46–59
Academic results, 108–132; and Army Revised Beta scores, 129–132; and curriculum level achieved, 115–119; and data-gathering procedures, 108–115; and educational behaviors, 115–122; and gain in IQ scores, 129–132; and number of active study hours, 119–120; and points earned for educational programs, 120–122; and retention data from follow-up study, 135–139; in specific curriculum areas, 128–129; and Stanford Achievement Test rates of gain, 122–129

Academic year, periods of, 111–115
ALEXANDER, M., xxiii
Alterations, tailoring, 156–157
Army Revised Beta, increased IQ scores in, 129–132
Auto-instruction, 47–49
AWOL, 33, 166
AYLLON, T., 5
AZRIN, N., 5

B

Banking system, 25–27, 155–156; loans from, 25–27, 155–156; savings and withdrawals from, 25, 155
Barbering facilities, 30, 67
"Bathroom syndrome," 83
Behavior: educational, 115–122; gathering reports on, 108–115
Behavioral approach to design of school facility, 37–40
BERBERICH, J. P., 5
BIS, J. S., 4

Index

Bonuses, 12–13, 32, 156
Books and library, 97–98. *See also* Library
BRIGGS, L. J., 48

C

Cafeteria. *See* Food service
CASE Interim Period, 60
CASE I pilot project, 4–5; subject matter of programed materials used in, 50
CASE II-MODEL project: academic level of students in, 3–4; basic premise of, 5–6; cultural and interpersonal results of, 81–107; daily routines in, 65–68; description of, 1–15, 153–155; evaluation of results of, 15, 139–142; follow-up study of, 133–142; general operation of, 60–80; influence of on public schools and training schools, 143; objectives of, 2–7; student orientation in, 62–65; students in, *see* Students; typical student's progress within, 68–80; use of money-points as reinforcers in, 7–9
CASE II Project Closing Period, 60
CASE II vs. National Training School, 144–151; offenses of students in, 145, 146; operating costs of, 150–151; operational comparisons of, 148–151; racial mix of students in, 147, 148; religious backgrounds of students in, 147, 148; staff of, 148–150; student populations of, 145–148

Chaplains, role of, 95–97
CHILDERS, A., xxiii
Church services, 174, 178
Classes, 52–53
COHEN, H. L., 4, 5, 38
COHEN, J. E., xxiii
COHEN, M. D., xxiii
Committee for Student Affairs, 31, 33, 34–35, 84, 86–87, 164, 165; and assisting adjustment of student to release, 92–94; and handling of homosexuality, 91

D

Daily routine, 65–68
Data-gathering procedures for academic results, 108–115
DE MEYER, M., 5
Dental services, 100–102, 168
Design, physical, of school, 37–46; behavioral approach to, 37–40
Dining facilities. *See* Food service
Dropouts, reasons for, 2–3
Dry cleaning and alterations, 156–157
DYRUD, J. E., 5

E

Educational area: procedures in, 157–162; hours of, 178–179
Educational behaviors, 115–122
Educational environment, 37–46; floor plans and design for, 43–45
Educational flow chart, 162
Educational program, 3–4, 9, 11, 46–59; academic results of, 108–132, 135–139; auto-instruction in, 47–49; behavioral objec-

Index

tives of, 109–110; classes in, 52–53; interviews with coordinator of, 54, 57, 58; learning and testing procedures in, 54–59, 157–162; programed courses in, 49–52; seminars in, 53–54

Emergency leaves, 26–27, 94

Environmental design, effects of on students, 81–87

Environmental feedback, 1–2

Environmental reinforcers, 16–36. *See also* Reinforcers

Experimental freshman year program at Southern Illinois University, xiv

F

Family contacts, 27–28

Federal Bureau of Prisons, 40, 105

FERSTER, C., 5

FILIPCZAK, J., 4, 5

Fines, 32–33, 162–163

Follow-up study, 133–142; and academic retention data, 135–139; contacting and interviewing for, 134–135; testing in, 135–139

Food service, 22–25, 40, 98–100, 156; and cafeteria hours, 177–178; for visitors, 27–28

G

Gates Reading Survey scores in follow-up study, 135–139

GERARD, R., xxiii

GEWISGOLD, H., xxiii

GLASER, R., 48

GOLDIAMOND, I., xxiii, 5

Grounds maintenance, 87

Group reinforcement, 12

H

Health program, 100–102, 168; and sick leave policy, 101

Home floor, 17–19

Homosexual rape, 88

Homosexuality, 89–91

I

Institutionalization, 91–92

Interviews with staff, 63–65, 163

IQ scores, gain in, 129–132

J

Jefferson Hall, plan of, 40–46, 163

Job training programs, 31–32

K

KIBLER, R., 5

Kitchen, 41–42

L

LARKIN, P., xxiii

Laundry facilities, 18, 163–164; hours and costs of, 179

Leaves, 164–166

Legal and Educational Alternatives to Punishment project (LEAP), 134

Leisure-time programs, 28–30, 169

Letter writing, 94, 167–168

LEVINSON, R., xxiii

Library, 29, 40, 42, 97–98, 160–161, 166–167; hours of, 179

Index

Living conditions, 13–14. *See also* Rooms, private
Lounge, 20–22, 40, 42, 167; improvement of social behavior in, 86–87
LOVAAS, O. I., 5
LUMSDAINE, A., 48

M

Mail procedures, 94, 167–168
Masturbation, 88
Medical services, 100–102, 168
MILES, D. A., 5
Money-points: as earned in educational programs, 120–122; rationale for use of, 7–9; use of as reinforcer, 7–9; uses for, 9, 16, 19–22
Movies, 29–30, 168
Music, 168–169

N

National Training School for Boys, Washington, D.C., 4, 6, 36, 62, 63; Federal/D.C. mix of students in, 61; food program of, 99, 100; handling of adolescent sexual behavior in, 87–88; handling of homosexuality in, 89, 90; homosexual rape in, 88; policy of on letter writing and visitors, 94–95; racial mix at, 61, 147, 148; recidivism rate at, 133; sick call at, 100
National Training School vs. CASE II, 144–151. *See also* CASE II vs. National Training School

O

Orientation to project, 62–65
Outdoor activities, 30, 169

P

Parole procedures, 169–170
Payroll procedures, 170–171
PERLOFF, B. F., 5
PETERSON, R. C., 48
Phone calls, 28, 171
PREMACK, D., 7
PRESSEY, S. L., 48
Pride of ownership, 85–86, 141
Private rooms, 13–15, 17–18, 38–39, 85–86, 106, 141, 176–177; rental rate for, 179
Private showers, 172, 179
Probation, 33
Programed courses, 49–52; assignment of point values to materials in, 51–52; CASE I experience with, 50; modification of publisher's, 50–51; subject matter of, 50; tests in, 51
Punishments, 32–33, 162–163

R

Racial adjustment, 83–85
Racial populations, 61, 84, 147, 148
Recidivism rate, 133–134, 135
Reinforcers: bonuses as, 12–13; environmental, 16–36; group, 12; money-points as, 7–9; private offices and bedrooms as, 13–

Index

15, 17–18, 85–86, 106, 141, 176–177; social (by staff members), 102–105; success of, 12, 141

Release: adjustment to, 91–94; programs for, 30–31, 172–173

Relief status, 6, 18–19, 173–174

Religious services, 174, 178

Rental items, 22

Restrictions, 174–175

Rooms, private, 13–15, 17–18, 38–39, 44, 85–86, 106, 141, 176–177; rental rate for, 179

S

SCHAEFFER, B., 5

Schools, public, projects similar to CASE II in, 143

Security system, students' interest in, 83

Self-instruction, 47–49; programs completed in, 117–119

Seminars, 53–54; hours of, 179

Sexual behaviors, 87–91

SHAH, S., xxiii

Shopping facilities, 16, 19–20, 21–22, 40, 181

Showers, private, 172, 179

SIDMAN, M., xxiii, 5

SKINNER, B. F., 48, 49

Social reinforcement of students by staff members, 102–105

Socialization of students, 105–107

Southern Illinois University, experimental freshman year program at, xiv

Sports program, 30, 169

Stanford Achievement Test: and gains in specific curriculum areas, 128–129; rates of gain in, 122–129; scores on in follow-up study, 135–139

STODDARD, L., 5

Store, 16, 19–20, 21–22, 40, 181; hours for, 179

Strike, student, 35–36

Student Educational Researcher, 9–11, 154–155, 157

Student Educational Researcher's Handbook, 10–11, 46, 63, 65; text of, 152–183

Student government, 33–36

Student strike, 35–36

Student workers, 31–32, 181

Students: adjustment of to release, 91–94; effects of environmental design on, 81–87; Federal vs. D.C. population of, 61–62; follow-up study on, 133–142; grounds maintenance by, 87; interviews of with staff members, 63–65, 163; offenses committed by, 62, 145; orientation of to project, 62–65; racial adjustment of, 83–85; racial populations of, 61, 84, 147, 148; recidivism rate of, 133–134, 135; on relief status, 6, 18–19, 173–174; sexual behaviors of, 87–91; social reinforcement of by staff members, 102–105; socialization of, 105–107; and testing battery, 64; typical progress of within project, 68–80

Survival cues, 1–2

191

Index

T

Tailoring alterations, 156–157

Teaching machine, 47–49

Telephone calls, 28, 171

Television room, 22

Tests of General Educational Development, National Training School, 15, 77

THORNDIKE, E., 48

Time cards and time clocks, 181–182

Trainees. *See* Students

Training school facility: behavioral approach to design of, 37–40; educational program of, 46–59; physical plan of, 40–46

Trips, 28

V

Visitors, 27–28, 94–95, 182; food services for, 27–28; visiting hours for, 179

Vocational classes, 182–183

Y

Youth Division parole authorities, review of student progress by, 65